BE YOUR OWN BOYFRIEND

Kaneisha

BE YOUR OWN BOYFRIEND

Decide to Be Happy, Unleash Your Sexy, and Change Your Life

KANEISHA GRAYSON

Manifesta Media
a division of Love & Achievement LLC | Austin, TX

In loving memory
of my high school sweetheart
and soul friend,
Joshua Aaron White,
who taught me how to love and how to let go

Dedicated to
my grandmother and confidante,
Evangelist Beulah Mae Sholtz,
who teaches me the importance of
self-love, surrender, and gratitude every day

A Note from the Author

This book is meant for inspiration and entertainment purposes for adults. It is not meant to replace medical or mental health treatment from a licensed professional.

Names and other identifying information have been included with permission or changed to preserve anonymity.

In writing this book, I have been influenced by a wide range of authors. I have made every effort to credit the people whose original ideas and concepts helped shaped this work. Throughout this book, I name the authors within the body of the book as well as in the list titled "Recommended Reading and Viewing" included in the appendix. Any incorrect attribution or failure to give proper credit where credit is due is unintentional, and will be corrected in subsequent printings.

If you acquired this book without paying for it, I'm not judging you! Such is the nature of our digital age. However, I would greatly appreciate it if you would consider leaving a thoughtful review of it online to help spread the word about the book. If you really enjoy it, please consider purchasing a copy for yourself or a friend.

Thanks for your attention and enjoy the book!

Acknowledgments

I am in awe of how many people had my back and were essential in getting this book out into the world. I want to thank my parents, John and Debra Grayson, for encouraging my dreams, embracing my adventurous spirit, and letting me find and pursue my own path. Thank you to my wonderful sister, Tameka Grayson, for your invaluable help with transcribing interviews and for always making me laugh and see the lighter side of life. I am inspired by the cheerfulness and calm you bring to any challenge, especially that of motherhood. I am so proud of you.

As mentioned in the dedication, my grandmother Beulah Mae Sholtz has served as my confidante and *Be Your Own Boyfriend* oracle for the past six years. Grandma, I thank you for never judging me and always making me feel understood. I hope my book makes you giggle while also making you proud—as our conversations usually do.

Thank you to my cousin, the young genius Johneesia Sholtz, for keeping me on track and serving as my mastermind partner. Millionaires-to-be unite!

Thank you to all of my closest and oldest friends who have loved me through the darkest "he's not The One" hours. The laughs, crazy stories, talking through movies, and Mexican Vanilla Amy's Ice Cream we've shared are some of my favorite memories. You make me so grateful that I returned home to Austin.

Thank you to my soul sisters and fellow woo-woo women around the world. You know who you are. You help me express Who I Really Am, and I am grateful for your friendship every day.

Thank you to all of my teachers and mentors—from Teri Road Daycare to J. Houston Elementary, Mendez Middle School, Kealing

Junior High, Johnston High School and the Liberal Arts Academy, Pomona College, University of Havana, University of Ghana, Harvard Kennedy School, and Harvard Business School—for expanding my mind and encouraging me to embrace my love of writing, creativity, and sharing. I consider teaching and working with young people to be the noblest of all professions, and I am deeply grateful to all of you.

To my coaching clients from the past three years without whom I would have had to get a "real" job and likely gotten distracted from the task of finishing this book, thank you for trusting me with your dreams. Never hesitate to let me know how I can support you as you pursue yours.

Thank you to all interns, coaches, freelancers, and team members I've ever worked with and especially to Catherine, Alexa, and Millie. You all lifted my spirits when I wanted to wallow in overwhelm. You gently brought me back to Earth when I wanted to board the "shiny new projects" spaceship. I am delighted to have you on my team and in my life.

Thank you to Andrés Salvador and the Fair Bean Coffee staff for making my writing den and second home tortilla-filled, empanada-tastic, and latte-licious. Keep brewing love and giving us writers a sun-drenched space with reliable wireless and plenty of outlets.

I am grateful for all the boyfriends, crushes, and missed connections I have had throughout my life. Each one of you has taught me something about myself, about life, and what it truly means to love myself.

Finally, my deepest gratitude goes to God for blessing me with the talent to write, the courage to share my gifts, and people in my life who appreciate and support my work.

Table of Contents

Introduction

*"You can search throughout the entire universe
for someone who is more deserving of your love
and affection than you are yourself,
and that person is not to be found anywhere.
You, yourself, as much as anybody in the entire
universe, deserve your love and affection."*
— GAUTAMA BUDDHA

LET'S GET ONE THING STRAIGHT: in no way am I trying to convince women to live without men. In fact, my desire to write *Be Your Own Boyfriend* was born out of my once lifelong obsession with finding my soulmate (or any mate for that matter) and getting married. I had been boy crazy since seventh grade, and—aside from a life-changing breakup in 2011—had never gone six months without a boyfriend. I've spent most of my twenties as the textbook case of the codependent woman. As I wrote this book, I realized I was exactly like the women I had decided to write the book for:

overly dependent on my relationship status for my sense of self-worth and obsessed with having a boyfriend when there were so many other parts of my life begging for my love and attention. So in case you are worried that my goal is to make men extinct, fear not. I want them around just as much as you do.

Nor is this book a "how to act happy and fabulous so you can catch a man" guide. Girl, you and I both know that attraction doesn't work that way. The woman who pretends to be happy, carefree, and excited about life while silently crying on the inside is even more repellent than the one with an obvious chip on her shoulder. I know because I've been that woman laughing on the outside and wailing *All By Myself*[1] on the inside. Pretending to be happy—whether it's to catch a man or to make a good impression on new people—is not fun, sustainable, or useful in helping you lead a happy life.

This book is a guide for women on how to experience an authentic and enduring *joie de vivre* that permeates her life whether or not she's in a relationship. *Be Your Own Boyfriend* is for the woman who wants to rewrite her story about life, love, achievement, relationships, and happiness. I gave my book a memorable title to constantly remind women to think, act, and feel as wonderful as they would feel if they had their dream relationship. The phrase "be your own boyfriend" is also a reminder that "like attracts like" and that if we want an amazing partner who adores us, we must first be willing to be and do that for ourselves.

---

[1] I'm referring to the Jewel version from *Clueless* where Cher is driving around and realizes she loves her stepbrother, Josh, though Celine Dion's version is amazing too.

This book will shed light on the unexpected threats to your happiness, explain why a healthy sense of sexuality matters, and empower you to be self-sufficient while being open to a relationship. Allow this book to guide you in transforming your life into all that you want it to be. To prove that "be your own boyfriend" is not just a catchy phrase but a mission statement you can live by, I've included stories from real women (and even some men!) who fell in love with their own lives first and then found The One. I've also collected tales from my readers and fans who have become significantly happier single people by experiencing the exhilaration of self-sufficiency, independence, and self-love.

To show that I, too, am on a journey of being my own boyfriend, I've included some of my intimate struggles in life and love in vignettes called Kaneisha Confessionals. I've also included accounts from dozens of men—happy husbands, smitten boyfriends, and hot singles—who weigh in on how attractive and downright necessary it is for the women in their lives to be independent and happy. I call those BYOB Brospectives. My friends and blog readers have generously shared their personal stories and self-love revelations in short features called Self-Love Stories and Self-Love Insights. Lastly, I've called upon happiness, dating, sex, and relationship experts to provide their best tips and strategies, which you can find labeled as BYOB Expert Advice throughout the book. I gathered a whole posse to show you how thrilling it can be to live by the BYOB code!

So as I hope you realize by now, I am writing to you not as a prim and proper expert, but as your outspoken and open-hearted sister in the journey to self-love. I was 80 percent done with the first draft of this manuscript when the man I thought was my future husband dumped me. Just five months prior to our devastating—but inevitable and much-needed—breakup, I had moved across the country to be closer to him. I had sold or left behind most of my belongings and bid adieu to my tiny apartment near Santa Monica Beach in California.

My boyfriend at the time (let's call him James) and I had been in a long-distance relationship for eight months when we decided to leave our respective cities and head to the Washington, DC area. At the time, James was unemployed in New York City, and I was just plain confused. I was self-employed as a graduate school admissions consultant while I wrote this book (or rather, while I procrastinated, complained, and agonized about how I didn't have enough time to write this book). After a year of being self-employed, I was baffled as to why my dreams of becoming a world-traveling writer and media personality had not yet materialized. I was utterly frustrated and completely clueless.

To make matters worse, I was blazing through my funds like the Beverly Hillbillies on payday. In the excitement of earning money as an entrepreneur for the first time, I didn't bother to save for the lean times—or even for my taxes. When I peeked through my fingers at my nearly empty checking account one sunny afternoon and realized that I couldn't afford to pay my rent, I knew I had to make a change.

Unfortunately, instead of changing my self-destructive habits or self-defeating thoughts, I changed coasts. I hastily agreed to a friend's generous offer to have me move into her new house and house-sit while she and her new husband were on their honeymoon. I frantically sold my furniture and prepared to move my entire life to the East Coast. Of course, this was after making sure James could move there with me—like any good codependent girlfriend would do. After nearly a year of being in a long-distance relationship, I was excited to finally live in the same city as my boyfriend. I fantasized about us conquering DC together as a power couple passionately in love. I was finally going to get my happy ending—or at least an ending to my (completely imagined) wretched state of singlehood!

Soon after we moved in together, our relationship unraveled into frequent and bitter arguments and smoldering grudges. James and I were two strong-willed people trying to smash our conflicting temperaments and different life visions together. Our dramatic not-quite-love story looked much more like a pilot for *The Real Housewives of Harvard* than the Barack-Michelle fairy tale we had both hoped to have. After four months, we finally decided (and by "we," I mean "he") that we did not belong together. Indeed, moving to DC resulted in an ending for us, but there was little that was happy about it.

When left unchecked, my tendency is to cling to relationships until the last drop of goodness has been squeezed out—until the relationship has disintegrated into lifeless dust. For most of my relationships, I have held on until one or both of us nearly hated each other. Even though I was desperately unhappy during the last few months of the relationship, I had still tried to convince myself that we could make our love (or toxic and codependent substitute for love) work.

Looking back, I realize that I was attached not to our relationship, but to an elaborate illusion (or rather, *delusion*) that I had created. Even though my money, happiness, and health were in shambles, I believed that being in a serious relationship in which we regularly discussed marriage meant that I was okay. I hate to admit it, but my whacked out rationale was, *If this man wants to be with me forever, then I gotta be doin' something right!*

Despite our glaring incompatibility, James and I had trudged on in the relationship far past its expiration date through months of counseling and countless fights. When he pulled the switch on our on-again, off-again relationship for the last and final time, I was devastated and exhausted. To my surprise, I was also extremely relieved.

I was free to be myself without apologizing for who I am or walking on eggshells. I was free to figure out what I really wanted in life rather than trying to squeeze my desires into someone else's vision. I was free from my compulsive need to control him, nag him, and try to make him depend on me emotionally. I was free to be happy—even if that meant being happy alone.

Despite the fact that I had spent a year working on a book titled *Be Your Own Boyfriend*, I had been doing anything but that. I had been using my relationship woes as a distraction from writing this book and building a business. Even though I'd had a great idea to write a book telling women to stop obsessing over their relationship status, I was still caught in my own painful, self-destructive cycle of codependency and addiction. Surely, my idea for this book was my subconscious crying out for help, and now that I was single, I could hear her loud and clear.

After James and I split up, a cloud of hopeless desperation lifted from my spirit. But then a cloud of loneliness moved into its place. After moving out of my friend's house, I moved to the nearby city of Baltimore, where I could actually afford the rent. In my completely new city, I had only one close friend nearby, and spent long days and nights alone since I worked from home. I often felt like a tribeless wanderer. On the other hand, the post-breakup months were also a liberating and enlightening period. Being alone allowed me to review the original manuscript of *Be Your Own*

Boyfriend and start taking my own advice to heart. Six months after moving to the East Coast, I decided to move back in with my parents in my hometown of Austin, Texas, and refocus on writing my book and building my business.

I began sending out a weekly email called *The Love Note* to approximately one thousand blog readers and coaching clients. In doing that, I found inspiration, a renewed sense of purpose, and a supportive community. Each week, I sent out a heartfelt message discussing my reflections on a pressing issue in my life or coaching business. These weekly emails gave me a chance to share my insights on love, achievement, and the pursuit of passion. I was buoyed by my readers' private email responses and their comments on my blog every week. They showed me that men and women around the world were grappling with the very same issues that were on my mind and in my heart. I wasn't alone. There were hundreds—if not thousands—of people around the world navigating the same troubled waters of adulthood.

As a single girl on a quest for balance and happiness, I saw my book with new eyes. I was able to chuck the fluff that didn't work, enhance the book with the lessons I was continually learning, get invaluable advice from friends and experts, and test my ideas as I developed them. I was finally making progress on my book, in my business, and in my life.

Even though I literally "wrote the book" on being your own boyfriend, it's still an ongoing struggle for me to prioritize my own health, happiness, and success over snagging a beau. However, the personal development and relationship experts, happily coupled folks, and thriving singles I connected with through writing this book have become my encouragement entourage as I walk the path of being my own boyfriend.

Throughout the book, you will notice that I direct my advice to straight women. Though I recognize how this language leaves out men and lesbian/bisexual/transgendered/queer women, I made the choice to write directly to straight women for the sake of simplicity and consistency. The message of *Be Your Own Boyfriend* is one that I hope resonates with people of all genders and sexual preferences. Anyone who wants to strengthen his or her self-love muscles can benefit from the insights in this book.

Though I have dedicated the last two years of my life to writing this book, my journey of being my own boyfriend isn't over. In fact, in many ways, it often feels as if I'm just beginning. I consider this book to be a battle cry to women across the world to stand up and join me. We can all encourage and support one another in being our best selves and living our best lives—whether we are in a romantic relationship or not.

Being in a healthy, committed relationship is still extremely important to me. I eagerly look forward to spending my life with someone who shares my life vision and understands, appreciates, excites, challenges, and inspires me. While writing this book, my heart and my mind transformed. I finally realized that the one constant companion I'll always have is myself—and if that relationship ain't right, no other one can be.

Be Your Own Boyfriend represents the best of what I have learned so far on my journey to self-love and independence. I know that there are precious gems of wisdom in here for every woman looking for a radical change in her life, and I am thrilled you have decided to join me. Let our journey begin!

Part 1:
Decide to Be Happy

Chapter 1:
Smiling through the Pain:
How Happy Are You?

*We can never obtain peace in the outer world
until we make peace with ourselves.*
— DALAI LAMA XIV

WHEN I'M IN LOVE, everything seems better somehow. A rainy day sets the stage for a romantic night in or better yet, a passionate kiss in the rain straight from the movies. However, when I've recently fallen out of love, a rainy day means annoying traffic, dangerously slick roads, and weird-smelling air. When I'm in love, sleeping through my alarm clock is a delightful reminder of the delicious night I had with my lover. When I'm not in love, waking up late leads to frantic rushing and a grumpy mood all morning. Living in love makes us feel hopeful, energetic, optimistic, and elated. We may even feel invincible! Living out of love makes us irritable, impatient, restless, and frustrated.

Everyone relishes the delirious happiness that comes with a new romance. However, if your joy and peace of mind depend primarily on your relationship status, beware! You are actually experiencing a deceptive, temporary euphoria rather than authentic, lasting happiness. Once you are no longer in the relationship, that blissful trance evaporates and leaves you feeling empty, lost, and out of control. The key is to learn how to harness that elusive "in love" power whether you are in a relationship or not. Being able to bask in the light of love regardless of your relationship status is the core principle of being your own boyfriend. What you so desperately seek in another person is already within you.

SELF-LOVE PRINCIPLE #1
**Real happiness comes from within
and is not based on the status of your romantic relationship.**

BYOB EXPERT ADVICE
So many of us are conditioned by society and our upbringing to look for love outside ourselves. And what we all know is that looking outside ourselves for love is a path to misery, a path to suffering.

— Christine Arylo, "Queen of Self-Love," inspirational catalyst, author of *Choosing ME before WE* and *Madly in Love with ME*

Know this: You don't have to wait for someone else to come along to hit the start button on your life. You can decide to have a life you love now—rather than in the future when you find The One or when the one you have becomes a better man. Making the decision to *be happy now* takes introspection, honesty, the courage to make life changes, and a commitment to your mental, physical, and emotional well-being. Most importantly, the decision requires the willingness to protect yourself from the elements that could erode your peace of mind.

Just as the first step to healing from addiction is to admit you have a problem, the first step in deciding to be happy is being honest with yourself. Look inside and ask yourself, *What areas of my life make me feel miserable or just plain glum?* Assess your daily life to see if the comfort of a relationship or the distractions of dating drama are keeping you from reaching clarity. Whether it's a sub-par social life, an unfulfilling job that saps your spirit, or an overly busy lifestyle that drains your joy, identify the areas of your life that need a happiness overhaul.

Have you ever had a persistent, dull ache—such as in your lower back—that never went away because you grew accustomed to it? Unhappiness in any area of your life can have the same damaging effect. Sometimes, it takes a drastic incident to jolt us into realizing that we are not happy.

BYOB EXPERT ADVICE

Christine Arylo tells the story of the drastic event that changed her life in 2001. At the time, she had a six-figure job and a big house. She was getting her MBA at the Kellogg Graduate School of Management at Northwestern and was about to get married. Everything seemed picture perfect, but it all fell apart one day.

On the way to our engagement party outside my mother's house, he stopped the car, looked at me, and said, "I don't love you. I don't want to marry you. And oh, by the way, I've been cheating on you for the last six months." That was my wake-up call. It was a big one. And I remember lying in bed a couple of weeks later, and this voice in my head said to me, "Christine, the hole in your heart isn't because he's not there; it's because you're not there."

SELF-LOVE PRINCIPLE #2

If you want others to love, appreciate, and respect you, you must love, appreciate, and respect yourself first.

At times, we are just going through the motions of everyday living, leading "lives of quiet desperation" as author Henry David Thoreau wrote. We unconsciously hope that tomorrow will magically bring a change, sadly believing deep down that everything will simply stay the same. Other times, it takes fully experiencing a moment of true joy to realize how unhappy we have been up to that point.

I'm not trying to make you feel dissatisfied or discontent with your life. I want to open your eyes to the reality that you may be ignoring a dull ache—not in your lower back, but in your heart. This persistent pain is your soul urging you to cultivate your happiness today rather than waiting for Mr. Right to start building a life you love.

When a Homeless Man Tells You to Smile—and Other Signs You Are Unhappy

1. You can't remember the last time you laughed really hard.

I don't care how busy you are or how quiet it is at your workplace. You should have at least one boisterous, semi-embarrassing guffaw every single day. If you are not giggling, chortling, or braying like a donkey at least once a day, you may be unhappy. Laughter feeds the soul, and cutting back on your daily giggles is one diet you will never need.

2. You have been unintentionally gaining or losing weight.

Food can often comfort us during stressful and emotionally trying times. Every woman loves an occasional organic dark chocolate bar seasoned by her freshly brewed tears. A bit of chocolate here and there is totally fine, but if your clothes are starting to get too tight (or far too loose), you may be guilty of emotional eating, neglecting your fitness routine, or restrictive dieting. Rushing from one appointment to the next also leads us to hastily eat fatty, processed meals or rely on fast food for fuel. Constantly having to eat in a rush, eating for comfort, and neglecting to exercise are sure signs of unhappiness.

KANEISHA CONFESSIONAL

I knew it was time for me to stop worrying about everything and start losing weight when I busted the zipper on three different dresses within three months. (One of those times, I was on a date on —guess what—Fat Tuesday!) Up until that point, I had been in denial about how pudgy I had become during the stressful last months of my relationship with James. After the third zipper-busting time, I vowed to stop eating out of boredom or sadness and get my butt back into the yoga studio. I'm still working on establishing a regular fitness routine, but thankfully, I'm no longer popping buttons off my pants or popping brownies mindlessly in my mouth.

3. Your friends are becoming standoffish.

People avoid those who kill the life of the party. If you feel like you aren't receiving as many social invitations as you'd like and people seem eager to get away from you, you may be broadcasting negative vibes. Whether it's incessantly complaining about your long list of troubles, engaging in mean-spirited gossip, or showing lack of interest in other people's stories, you could be committing social gaffes. You may not have realized it yet, but you could be "that girl" at the party that makes people squirm. If you recognize yourself in any of the aforementioned no-no behaviors, you may be radiating unhappy vibes and destroying your social life.

4. You have physical pain or keep getting sick.

If you have been experiencing neck pains, stomach pains, migraines, severe cramps, back pains, inexplicable rashes, or suffer from a recurring cold, your shrouded misery could be compromising your health. Since our minds and bodies are intimately connected, your body is likely demonstrating physical manifestations of emotional and spiritual pain. They may be symptoms of a serious illness I call sad-itis.

KANEISHA CONFESSIONAL

After one particularly painful breakup, I cried for days, and then I broke out in shingles! (Pause for a stomach-churning Google Images search to get a quick glimpse at shingles. Crazy, right?) The shingles started as a deep muscle pain on the left side of my neck. It felt as if the day before, I had participated in a competitive weightlifting contest using only my neck muscles, and then slept on a boulder as a pillow that night. Next, a burning rash formed behind my left ear and snaked all the way down the left side of my neck. I realized that in the wake of my breakup, I wasn't only crying from my eyes; my body was crying from the inside out!

5. You don't sleep well.

Your racing mind keeps you awake for hours. You suffer from insomnia. You have recurring nightmares. Or you wake up exhausted. Even when you get plenty of sleep (and perhaps you often oversleep), you don't feel refreshed in the morning. You often feel like you need to sleep one more night—or even three—to function normally during the day. If this is how you feel, you are most likely unhappy.

I am not a doctor or therapist, but I believe that many of the signs of deep melancholy and suffering that Western society labels as depression could be solved with a healthier diet, consistent exercise, and some prayer or meditation. I have lost people that I love to depression and other mental illnesses. I fully acknowledge that clinical depression is real, and I'm so grateful that we have scientific advances to treat mood disorders. However, all too often, our spirits are sick—not our minds.

There is no shame in admitting to yourself that you aren't as happy as you would like to be. Being honest with yourself about how you really feel is the first step to awakening to the tremendous happiness that already lives within you and is just waiting for you to let it out.

SELF-LOVE PRINCIPLE #3

**Listen to what your mind, body, and spirit are telling you
about your happiness or lack thereof.
Once you start listening and stop ignoring,
you can start reclaiming your joy, health, and peace of mind.**

Chapter 2:
Facebook Frenemies
and Other Threats
to Your Happiness

Happiness is when what you think, what you say,
and what you do are in harmony.
— MAHATMA GANDHI

BEFORE MOVING ON to how to bring more joy, calm, and fulfillment in your life, I want to discuss the unexpected but insidious threats to your happiness. These joy-stealing culprits are hidden everywhere around us, and it's up to you to keep them in check.

Happiness Threat #1:
Social Media Stalking and Stuntin'

Social media can be a convenient way to engage with our friends and family, share information, and connect with like-minded folks around the world. However, it also lures us out of the present into a fast-paced virtual environment where everyone is performing a highly curated online identity behind the mask of a computer screen. The personas we project online are not who we really are. They are who we want people to *think* we are—not quite our "best selves," but our best imitation of who and what we think others want us to be. Just think about it: When you post a status update on Facebook, the point is to be noticed and "liked" by others. If people "like" their own status, we roll our eyes and think they are corny for doing so. So much of not-so-social media is about getting other people to approve of you rather than approving of yourself.

There is nothing wrong with working to present your reflected best self in your online activities. The danger is in thinking that a social media stream represents an "accurate" representation of someone's daily life. When we spend too much time on social media, we constantly compare ourselves to other people, trying to make our online selves cooler, smarter, more interesting, funner, more informed, more adventurous, and more in love than our "friends." We use our great jobs, fabulous engagement rings, adoring romantic partners, cute babies, and lavish international adventures as props in our self-promotion efforts.

The sad consequence of spending too much time in the 24/7, energized, electrified world of social media is you begin to devalue the present moment. For example, rather than enjoying the scenic view on your whale-watching cruise, you're hastily snapping pictures to post on Instagram or racking your mind for a clever tweet about the experience. You end up living for other people's likes and retweets rather than for your own self-expression and happiness.

BYOB EXPERT ADVICE

It's really important for people to just remember who they are and be authentic to themselves. Social media is great, and it can be a lot of fun. But if you start to get into that place where you're spinning in that hole because you see all these negative things, just step away from that. Focus on the people that are present with you and be present with those people.

— Denise Antoon, President of PR and social media firm Antoon Group

All of this clamoring for attention and approval gives our power away to the external world, rather than allowing us to be our own biggest fans, best friends, and support system.

SELF-LOVE PRINCIPLE #4

When you are your own biggest fan, other people's opinions about your life matter far less.

Happiness Threat #2:
Glossy Mags That Make You Feel Gross
and Mean Girl Entertainment "News"

Copious airbrushing and endless pages of ads for luxury items scream to magazine readers, "YOU AREN'T GOOD ENOUGH . . . unless you buy this $5,000 purse." Daily celebrity gossip shows spotlighting the lavish vacations, scandalous extramarital affairs, and bitter, protracted celebrity divorces normalize drama and excess. Rather than being horrified by the soul-destroying misery broadcasted in the mass media, we eagerly lap it up, attracting a pared-down version of the celebrity drama into our own lives.

While fashion magazines and celebrity gossip can be an entertaining way to wind down after a long day, those outlets often leave behind seeds of discontent for their consumers. The advertisers in fashion magazines and entertainment news programs push the idea that not only can everyone be a celebrity of some sort —you should want to act, live, and shop like a celebrity.

After twenty minutes engrossed in a high-end fashion magazine, you may end up feeling fat, plain, and poor when you are actually a beautiful, interesting, financially independent woman. Enjoy your magazines and celebrity gossip in moderation. If you don't take any of it too seriously, it can be very entertaining. But don't let the bright lights, glossy spreads, sensational stories, and skilled airbrushing fool you into hating your body or your life.

Happiness Threat #3:
Comparing Yourself to Others

It's natural to compare ourselves to people of the same age group or educational background and then think about how we measure up. (Comparalisha[2] rolls her eyes and says, "Oh, she has her own column at *The Huffington Post*? Well, no wonder. Her boyfriend's sister is an editor there. If I was banging the editor's brother, I would have a column there too!") Whether you compare yourself to friends or strangers, you never win. The tendency when comparing is to look for flaws in others, which always makes you feel like crap because you eventually start obsessing over the flaws in yourself. Comparing ourselves to other people is always a lose-lose situation that turns others into villains and you into a victim. This scarcity-driven worldview makes you feel more alienated from others rather than more connected. Thinking this way only serves to make us all feel more fearful, desperate, greedy, and suspicious of others. It perpetuates a feeling of lack, which only attracts more reasons to feel lack into your life. When you notice that you are comparing yourself (favorably or unfavorably) to another person, turn your attention to something more loving. You can reflect on how grateful you are to know someone doing such great things or think of how you can be helpful to someone trying to reach a goal you have already attained.

---

[2] Comparalisha's mean girl posse includes Ensequritee, LoSelphasteem, and Djustahater (the D is silent).

SELF-LOVE PRINCIPLE #5

**You have the power to validate your own
feelings, thoughts, experiences, and accomplishments.
Your life is unique and can't be compared to anyone else's.**

KANEISHA CONFESSIONAL

When I started to share with friends and family that I wanted to try pursuing a career as a motivational speaker and author, most people responded with an excited "Ooh, you're going to be the next Oprah!" For a while, I delighted in this comparison because it meant they believed that I could achieve a modicum of the success, influence, and wealth that Oprah has in her lifetime. However, the comparison became a heavy burden after a while. It got to the point where I would be faced with a career decision and think, "What would Oprah do?"

After about a year, I realized how toxic it was for me to compare myself to Oprah and to let other people do so as well. It was causing me to try and reverse-engineer someone else's journey to success rather than forge my own path through hard work, perseverance, and heeding my intuition. Now when people compare me to Oprah, I politely smile and say, "Nope, I'm Kaneisha." Though I deeply respect Oprah's journey and what she stands for—and would LOVE to meet and collaborate with her one day (Hey, Oprah! I'm free and ready whenever you need me!)—I'm not "the next Oprah" or the next anybody else. I'm the one and only Kaneisha Grayson.

Everyone is on a unique journey in life. You can't walk someone else's path and call it your own. Comparing yourself to others is fruitless because there will always be someone who is thinner, stronger, smarter, richer, prettier, and more popular than you. Rather than be discouraged by that fact, be relieved. You are perfect in your imperfection.

A SELF-LOVE STORY

I started to feel the pressure when I was twenty-five years old, when most of my classmates from high school and college were engaged, married, or having babies, and I wasn't even near ready for any of that. I started to feel panicky, measuring my life against theirs. It didn't serve me to do that because my life and my path were very different than the ones that they had. It didn't make theirs worse or better than mine or vice versa. It just meant that it was different.

— 34 years old, Austin, TX, single

You're only one person. Live your life in the colors, sounds, and textures that suit you. When we focus on using our own measuring stick for our lives, we can get clear on what we truly want in life and set the intention of attracting those things to us.

BYOB EXPERT ADVICE

Be the first person to validate your worth in the morning and the last before you go to bed.

— Debra Grayson, founder of decor and event services company Bedazzled by Debra (and my mother!)

Happiness Threat #4:
Second Helpings at the Bad News Buffet

The saying "You are what you eat," should apply to everything we consume—not just food. In my teens and early twenties, I indulged in a lot of cultural darkness: depressing movies, sad music, disturbing art. I spent hours hanging out in dimly lit coffee shops— like I imagined a writer would, though I wasn't doing any writing. I wasn't a particularly unhappy person; I just considered sad things to be so much "deeper" and thought-provoking. Rather than question my attraction to depressing things, I heralded my penchant for melancholy as an appreciation for high art and culture.[3]

I'm still drawn to tearjerker films, twisted psychological thrillers, and sad, soulful music, but I balance that with a healthy appreciation of stand-up comedy, upbeat dance jams, feel-good films, and goofy laughs from YouTube videos and Internet memes. Everything that you consume—what you read, what you watch on television, what you eat—becomes part of you. Just like we all have different metabolism rates, we all digest media in different ways. Art of all kinds deeply affects me—both positively and negatively— so I have to be very careful about what I give my time, emotional energy, and attention to. Just as consuming too many banana splits and pepperoni pizzas will weigh you down, so will consuming too much sadness and negativity. Remember: you can be a smart and cultured woman—and happy too!

---

[3] During my "emo" years, I refused to watch any movie whose DVD cover didn't feature award laurels (the leaves that frame the title of an independent film award). To say the least, I was a very annoying person to accompany to the video store.

SELF-LOVE PRINCIPLE #6
**Anything that you pay attention to has the power
to influence your thoughts, your feelings, and your life.
Feed your mind, body, and soul with inspiration and positivity.**

Happiness Threat #5:
Self-Limiting Talk

Here are some examples of self-limiting talk:

- "Black/Arab/Asian/Indian/White/Latina/etc. women don't do stuff like that."

- "Big girls really should not . . . "

- "Smart women shouldn't have to . . . "

- "You know I could never . . . "

- "Where I come from, people don't . . . "

- "If I were smarter/thinner/younger/more educated/more experienced, maybe I would try . . . "

Self-limiting talk is a sneaky little bastard that pops up in many situations: when we are shopping for new clothes, making our career goals, commenting on a TV show, or simply sitting around talking with our girlfriends. Just like the incessant chatter running through our minds, self-limiting talk is natural for most of us. We think we are innocently stating a personal preference or just being "realistic." However, when we make prescriptive statements like those above, we imprison ourselves. We tell ourselves who we can't be, what we can't do, and what we'll never be able to do. In effect, we put restrictions on ourselves instead of blowing the lid off of what is possible and proudly proclaiming all that we can be, do, and achieve.

The next time you hear yourself or someone else use self-limiting talk, stop and say, "You know, I used to think that way, but now I realize that idea is something I believed out of habit. I don't actually believe that!"

When you refuse to engage in self-limiting talk or catch yourself mid-sentence, you will instantly feel better. You will also influence those around you to move away from self-limiting talk and toward self-empowering talk. As you move to adopting self-empowering talk, there is no need to lecture others on their self-limiting talk. By pumping yourself up through the words you use, you will subtly inspire others to do the same.

When you set the example of refusing to engage in self-limiting talk, this habit will eventually all but disappear from your environment. This may take time, so be patient. We all learned to engage in some form of self-limiting talk because it has been repeated to us (either in our own heads or by other people) enough times until we believed it. While you can't control your friends and colleagues, you have complete control over what comes out of your own mouth. Make sure your words serve to lift you up rather than knock you down.

SELF-LOVE PRINCIPLE #7
**Use the power of your words to make your world
an abundant place of possibility.**

Happiness Threat #6:
Expectations for How Things "Should Be"

You can make yourself very miserable playing the "should" game. I'm sure you've all heard these common occurrences of the "shoulds":

- I should be married by now.

- I should be further in my career by now.

- I should own a house by now.

- I should weigh less than this.

- My relationship isn't working, but it should be.

Similar to self-limiting talk, clinging to expectations of the way your life should be ruins your enjoyment of your life as it really is. I'm not saying that you have to pretend to be 100 percent satisfied with every part of your life. We all have circumstances in our lives we wish were different. However, being hard on yourself because things haven't worked out the way you expected gets you nowhere.

BYOB EXPERT ADVICE

I was one of those people who planned, planned, planned and had a checklist about the kind of life and job I wanted, when I needed to get married—all that kind of stuff. And then everything in my life came crashing down. I had left my career that I had worked so hard to achieve. I was dealing with tons of debt. I was estranged from my family at the time. I was dealing with major health issues. And my fiancé had just broken up with me six months before my wedding.

So there were a lot of times when I was screaming into a pillow because I was so angry. There were a lot of times I was crying myself to sleep. I was doubting God. There were a lot of times where I so wanted to eat a pint of ice cream or drink a bottle of wine to make it go away. And they were so many times I wanted some guy to come in and rescue me.

But I had tools. And I think that's what it's really about. We don't just wake up one day and everything shifts. We wake up, we have the awareness, and then we have to practice changing in the moment by choosing different tools. So I had lots of coaches and lots of training. These are the tools I learned from the most: (1) really paying attention to my thoughts, challenging them, and going, "Is that thought true?" and (2) freeing myself of judgment. I think forgiveness is really the key to freedom. I mean, that's how it was for me: forgiving myself, forgiving others, and really allowing myself to be guided rather than trying to plan everything out.

— Christine Hassler, inspirational speaker, life coach, author of
The 20 Something Manifesto and *20 Something, 20 Everything*

Happiness Threat #7:
Ungratefulness

I think that ingratitude could be the root of all unhappiness. Taking the time to appreciate all the good things in your life shifts your attention away from problems and focuses it on the many blessings you have. Your attention on those blessings draws more of them to you. On the other hand, constantly noticing what's wrong with your life, dwelling on what's missing, and feeling cheated will give you even more woes to complain about.

Here's one quick and easy cure for ingratitude: every time you feel inclined to complain, go in the opposite direction. Say out loud something you are thankful for. There are so many ways to exercise your appreciation muscles.

BYOB BROSPECTIVE

Get a bowl and write down every time you're grateful for something over the course of the day and put it in the bowl. And at the end of the week, look at that bowl and say, "Well, look how much I had to be grateful for all week." Might change your perspective a little bit.

— Eric Handler, cofounder of PositivelyPositive.com

Soon enough, you'll be too busy being grateful to let your happiness seep away.

SELF-LOVE PRINCIPLE #8
**Release expectations for how your life "should be"
and be grateful for the blessings you have in your life
right now.**

Happiness Threat #8:
Thinking You Can Change Circumstances
or People That You Can't

Self-empowerment and determination only go so far. Sometimes, we can do ourselves and others a great disservice by thinking that we have the power to change circumstances that we simply have no ability to control. Whether it's a boyfriend who you wish would be more assertive or your mom who you wish would be less controlling, you don't have the ability to control other people— even if you *think* you know what's best for them. Trying to fix other people's problems will surely erode your happiness and destroy your relationships. Often, we use "helping" others as an excuse not to focus on our own lives.

KANEISHA CONFESSIONAL

When I first discovered my passion for reading personal development books, I did a great job of knowing what I was supposed to do but a horrible job of actually taking the advice to heart. For example, if my guy hadn't called me in two days, instead of doing what I knew I should do—go on about my life, being happy and enjoying my own company—I would start to freak out, wondering if he had skipped out on me. I would start scheming up ways I could turn the balance of "relationship power" back to my side. It took me a few years to realize that belief happens on two levels: our words and our actions. I was reading and saying all the right affirmations that I learned in my self-help books, but my actions were full of fear and doubt. Once I started actively following the advice I proclaimed to believe in, I was much happier, more at peace, better able to deal with uncertainty, and more secure in relationships. I also stopped buying so many self-help books once I realized that all I needed to do was follow the good advice in the books I already owned.

By consistently matching your outwardly positive actions with inwardly positive thoughts, you'll work out your happiness muscles. Soon enough, joyfulness will no longer be an elusive state you strive for; it will be your natural default.

Chapter 3:
Happiness Is a Choice

Your thoughts and your feelings create your life.
It will always be that way. Guaranteed.
— LISA NICHOLS

WE ALL WANT HAPPINESS so badly that we tend to give it a magical quality. We often think of it as something that *happens* to us. You might fantasize about the elation you would feel if you won the lottery or if the man you've been eyeing at the library swept you off your feet. Yes, happiness is something we can experience due to our circumstances, but it's more than that. Happiness is a way of being. It doesn't just happen to you, and it's certainly not some elusive gift that is hiding from you; it's the choices we make every day, the actions we take, and the thoughts and beliefs we hold. Even when things don't turn out as you expected or hoped, you can still choose to have a light and happy heart. The skeptic in you might be giving you the side-eye, thinking this sounds simplistic and overly optimistic. Just give her a cup of Earl Grey and tell her to sit down somewhere. I promise you that it can be just that easy. The simple strategies in this chapter will help you claim your happy and stay that way.

Choose Your Problems Wisely

One evening, I was having dinner with my good friend Laura, a wildly successful Internet entrepreneur who is constantly making decisions about her growing business. Laura and I love getting together and talking about business and boys over a scrumptious meal. This particular day, she had a rough time at work and was venting. Similarly, I was rambling about all my financial worries and career angst. In the midst of our vent session, I stepped back and realized that, although we were both dealing with challenges, we both felt capable of handling them. The problems we were facing had no real influence or power over our futures. If these weren't the types of problems we wanted, we could simply make different choices going forward and choose to have new problems. In fact, in that moment, I had this realization about happiness and choices:

SELF-LOVE PRINCIPLE #9
**Happiness is not the absence of problems.
It's about choosing which types of problems you want
and feeling empowered to accept and address them.**

For example, I used to think that all my problems would magically be solved (or magically not matter anymore) once I found a man to sweep me off my feet. It's naïve, I know, but countless women consider finding The One as their life plan (and life jacket) all the time. However, being in a relationship can often be more difficult than being single because you're balancing the needs, wants, and idiosyncrasies of two people rather than just your own. When you have a boyfriend, fiancé, or husband, all your problems don't magically dissolve; you just have a different set of challenges.

As you move through life, in and out of various stages of relationships, you take your current problems and trade them in for different ones. Of course, there are some problems like dishonesty that may follow you wherever you go—no matter how much you try to trade up. That's why you have to be sure that you're not running from your current problems. Face your problems and decide whether you'll address them or let them go. That way, they won't haunt you as you move into the next stage of your life.

BYOB BROSPECTIVE

The most attractive woman believes that problems have solutions. She has plans to make things how she wants them to be. In other words, attractiveness means never giving up and having a cool, calm, positive outlook.

— 26 years old, Gaithersburg, MD, in a relationship

Make Decisions That Protect Your Happiness

Our life is made up of a million decisions we make each day that build upon and affect one another. Though some decisions are more significant than others, each one has the ability to nurture your happiness or hinder it. Be sure that when you are making decisions large and small, you are considering their potential impact on your happiness. Here's a quick guide:

1. Listen to your intuition.

As you face decisions, be still enough to allow your intuitive knowing to emerge. Be willing to listen and follow where it guides you. Daily meditation is a great way to create the space for you to hear your intuition. Even just ten minutes of quiet stillness each morning and/or evening can give you tremendous benefits through stress relief, clearing your mind, and letting your good ideas surface.

2. Consider doing what you would do if failure was not a possibility.

Nobody wants to try something and fail at it, but fear of failure keeps most people from taking even the first step toward a goal they have. Only the people who actually take risks have the privilege of failing. Everyone else is just standing on the sidelines watching, waiting for the perfect moment to act.

3. Do what you would do if no one would be mad or disappointed.

It's natural to care about what our friends, family, and colleagues think of us. For example, I am highly motivated by pleasing others and receiving their admiration and praise. My tendency to yearn for external approval often ends up getting me all mixed up in the head when it's time to make a decision. I try to find a perfect solution where my problem gets fixed and no one is inconvenienced or upset about it. In short, I tend to search for a guarantee that no one will criticize me. But as we all know, the only guarantee in life is that one day, we will all leave this Earth. Considering that you get this one precious life (at least in this incarnation anyway), you should spend it doing what your heart, in partnership with good sense, leads you to do rather than making decisions to seek others' approval.

It took me years to learn this central lesson from Melody Beattie's breakthrough book *Codependent No More*:

> *You can't take care of yourself and*
> *another person's feelings at the same time.*

Rather than putting other people's feelings and opinions above your own well-being, make your decisions without worrying about people being mad or disappointed that you didn't do what they wanted. It is possible to be considerate of other people's feelings without letting them matter more than your own.

SELF-LOVE PRINCIPLE #10
**Trying to please everyone is impossible and
undermines the power of your own inner compass.**

4. Pretend that no one is going to congratulate you on your decision.
Similar to the last point, if you are a person who thrives from receiving gold stars for your accomplishments, you probably look for ways to get attention, respect, and maybe even envy from your friends. While it may feel good in the moment to make someone go, "Ooh, look at her. She's so fancy," you are ultimately the one who will live with the consequences of your decision. Don't make your decisions based on the people you hope to impress, how many "likes" you'll get on Facebook, or how many high fives you will slap at the next happy hour. If you make decisions that support your personal and professional goals, I promise you'll get the delicious and irreplaceable stamp of approval from your own intuition. That's the only one that truly matters.

5. Share your decision with someone after sleeping on it.
After you have taken time to properly think through a decision, its possible consequences, and what path would make you most happy, give yourself some time to have that decision be yours and yours alone. You can be scared about the future and still feel like you are making the right decision. Once you have digested it, if you still feel good about it, share the news with a trusted friend. This will help make the decision seem more real and create some accountability.

KANEISHA CONFESSIONAL

After months of going back and forth in my head and with my team, I finally decided to combine my dating and happiness blog and my admissions consulting blog under one united website. My intuition was screaming, "This is what you need to do!" but I was still terrified. I feared that my graduate school applicants would be put off by the lifestyle content and that my lifestyle blog readers would be bored by the admissions information. Even though I wasn't sure how I was going to make it work, I knew deep inside that it was time to stop splitting my world in half and move forward with one website.

I drafted a long and heartfelt letter to my mailing list about my decision to merge my interests in personal and professional development into one site, and had the email send out while I was sleeping. It felt great waking up to a new reality: I was now responsible for running one business: the business of being me. The road ahead wasn't clear, but I was confident that I had made a decision in line with my intuition.

The name of my company with a newly combined focus was Love & Achievement LLC. The name perfectly captured the mission of my two prior websites and more importantly, my two areas of expertise.

A year after making that decision, I am thrilled that I took a leap of faith. My business is stronger than ever, my audience is growing every day, and my energies are no longer split between two websites. Having one website that combines two seemingly incongruent areas has given me the confidence to keep evolving and pivoting my business as my interests and skills change. I am so grateful that I listened to my intuition rather than succumbing to my fear.

6. Serious decisions require at least a one-week waiting period.

When I'm very stressed about a particular decision, I can be very indecisive, swinging wildly from one option to the other. This indecision likely comes from a fundamental lack of trust in myself to know what is best for me. Excitable and fickle can be a dangerous combination, especially when I think out loud with other people and drag them through the rollercoaster in my head. What's worse, the conflicting opinions I solicit from other people clutter my vision even more. I've discovered that sticking to a mandatory waiting period before publicly declaring or acting on a big life decision allows me to be confused in peace.

Just Breathe . . . Act As If Everything Is Already Okay

Despite all the tools, strategies, and mood-boosting activities you try, sometimes there are problems that you just can't solve in the moment. So you begin to tweak out and freak out. Maybe you fret by emotional eating, repeatedly refreshing your email inbox ("Maybe the answer will rain down on me from the gmail gods!"), or talking endlessly with a friend about the issue. Acting as if everything is already okay is not about being in denial; it's about realizing that you don't always immediately have the answer you seek but that you can at least be happy and at peace while the answer makes its way to you. It's about letting go and trusting that God, the Universe, and your intuition will deliver the answer to you when you need it.

Regardless of the hours I have spent searching for answers, researching online, worrying, and wringing my hands, a good long freak-out has never solved my problems. What always helps, however, is releasing the need to worry and making the decision to go on about the business of living my life. Once I was more relaxed and less focused on all the unresolved issues, I was able to think more clearly and identify possible solutions. Once I let go, the solutions became clear to me. They were previously out of my reach because I was blinded with worry, doubt, and fear.

The next time you have a problem weighing you down, do your best to address the problem, recognize when you've hit your limit, and then act as if all is well. Go about your life as if you did not have the problem, knowing that the solution is on its way. The answer will eventually emerge. It will likely be one of those "duh!" moments when you realize the answer to your question was a simple solution sitting in plain sight, patiently waiting for you to notice.

It's okay to take time to think through problems and identify possible solutions, but don't let fruitless worry and overthinking consume you. When you focus too much on solving problems, you undermine your happiness.

SELF-LOVE PRINCIPLE #11
**Do your best to solve your problems and then
trust that the Universe will take you the rest of the way.
Act as if everything is already okay.**

Chapter 4:
Learn to Let Go

Some people believe holding on
and hanging in there are signs of great strength.
However, there are times when it takes much more
strength to know when to let go and then do it.
— ANN LANDERS

THE WORST BREAKUPS of my life have always been the result of one of us (usually me) refusing to let go. Deep unhappiness sets in when we are trying to hold on to a relationship that no longer serves us. Sometimes, it's difficult for us to comprehend that the other person wants to be let go. Since the people we spend most of our time with have a huge influence on our mental and emotional state, learning to let go of rotting relationships is essential to nurturing and protecting your happiness.

BYOB EXPERT ADVICE

Oftentimes, we choose to stay in certain relationships because we think that's where our love is coming from. Our partner becomes our source of love. When that happens, we settle for what we have, and we stop pursuing the lives we really want.

— Christine Arylo, "Queen of Self-Love," inspirational catalyst, author of *Choosing ME before WE* and *Madly in Love with ME*

When a relationship has run its course, many of us tend to reminisce in our heads about how wonderful and exciting the relationship once was. Rather than face the truth of how unfulfilling our current situation is, we yearn for the past, oftentimes editing the past in our mind, making the relationship seem better than it really was. With the right amount of "selective remembering," a stressful, conflict-ridden, toxic relationship can be reimagined as a passionate but doomed love affair. When it comes to relationships, it's best that you have your eyes wide open about the reality of how well your relationship is really going.

BYOB BROSPECTIVE

I always say, "Relationships are like a mountain." First, when the relationship starts, it just keeps going up. You meet each other and have that honeymoon stage. And then once you hit the apex of the mountain, things start to get real, and you start to learn about that person. A good relationship stays at the apex. You obviously may come down a little, but you basically always stay close to the top.

But then, for some relationships, when you start to really find out who that person is and you don't like what you're seeing, you start backsliding down the mountain. But the problem is that since you've been to the mountaintop, you know that you can be at the mountaintop with that person. So you always keep fighting, thinking, "Don't worry, I'll slide back up." And you don't slide back up. The only way is down.

— Lincoln Anthony Blades, author of *The Myth of the Multiple Orgasm*, blogger at ThisIsYourConscience.com

Don't get fooled into staying in a damaging relationship just because you can see the apex of the mountaintop of your relationship. ("If he would just stop cheating, lying, and drinking so much, I just know we could be blissfully happy!") A *potentially* good relationship and one that actually *is* healthy, happy, and empowering are two completely different animals. You don't want to waste your life, waiting for a relationship—or a man—to reach a point of potential. Don't pretend you have a war horse when all you really have is a jackass.

Letting Go Reluctantly:
When He Says He Doesn't Know What He Wants

Some of the most dreaded words in a relationship are "We need to talk." It always means you're about to get the breakup talk. I know this statement well. After all, I've said and heard it many times! But there's another all-too-familiar statement that has left me confused, angry, and heartbroken:

"I'm not sure what I want right now."

What you mean you ain't sure what you want right now?! That's what I scream inside my head when I hear those words. In the past, hearing this sentence made me want to hurl something large, expensive, and fragile across the room (or at the man who said it). But I've learned a lot since my dating dummy days in my teens and early twenties. I now realize that rather than spinning into a blind rage, women must have a clear plan of action when a man says he doesn't know what he wants.

I once considered this statement a cop-out, a line guys used so they could continue sleeping with you without having to commit to you. For some guys, that's exactly what it is. However, after copious reading, reflection, trial and error, and hundreds of testimonials from my blog readers, I now know what the dreaded phrase means. "I don't know what I want right now" is often how a man expresses his genuine ambivalence about the relationship. One possible reason you might hear this phrase is that your man realizes that you know exactly what you want, and he cannot—or is not willing to—give you what you want. Rather than saying, "I'm never going to call you my girlfriend," or "Look, I'm just not going to marry you —ever," he says he doesn't know what he wants. It's easier for him. He hopes that you will get the hint and understand that this relationship is not going any further.

Most often, when a guy says he doesn't know what he wants, he is gently communicating, "I'm not sure that I want to be in an exclusive relationship with you." Or worse, he is giving a sheepish euphemism for the more painfully direct statement, "I *do not* want to be in a relationship with you." Go ahead, ask any guy and he'll tell you what's up.

BYOB BROSPECTIVE

"I don't know what I want." If I say that, most of the time, it means "I don't want to be with you."

— 28 years old, Los Angeles, CA, dating

TIME FOR A QUIZ, LADIES!

After several months of dating, if a guy says that he doesn't know what he wants, should you:

a) Scream, "But I already told everyone you were The One! What will everyone think if we break up now?!" Surely, he will then realize that this relationship is *on*—whether he wants it to be or not.

b) Deliberately outline for him all the reasons why the two of you should stay together. Let him know that you are willing to carry the burden of making the relationship work. With your help, he'll see more clearly what a huge mistake he is about to make.

c) Calmly say, "I understand. Take as much time as you need to figure out what you want. I know that I want an exclusive relationship. If you aren't sure that's what you want, then you should take some time to figure that out." Then go about your life as a newly single woman.

If you chose option A, you are a Catastrophe Queen, the kind of woman that has a meltdown at the first sign of relationship trouble. Even though it is the exact opposite of what you were trying to accomplish, you have successfully run him off. When men say the dreaded statement, it is likely because they are overwhelmed by the attention and intensity the woman is bringing to the relationship. All you have done with that outburst is make him *more* uneasy about being in a relationship with you.

If you chose B, you are what I call the Perfectly Reasonable Dater. You think it's "perfectly reasonable" that he doesn't know what he wants, and that it's "perfectly reasonable" for you to compile a list of the reasons why you two belong together forever. You think that if you can just convince him that you alone can fix the relationship, he will see the light. The Perfectly Reasonable Dater is the same woman who always seems to find a "perfectly reasonable" explanation for why none of her relationships work out. *He has abandonment issues. You know, because his mom lost him at the grocery store when he was six. He just needs to know that I'll never leave him, and then he will be ready to commit.* No, no, no! Your job is not to be his mother, his therapist, or the midwife to his unbirthed emotions. Your job in a relationship is to present your most authentic, happy, and healthy self to another person, and to be willing to accept and love the other person. If he doesn't want that level of commitment, isn't ready for it, or just can't see how great you two could be together, it is not your job to convince him, help him prepare, or show him the way to loving you.

Brainy girls tend to fall in the trap of being the Perfectly Reasonable Dater. With the help of my well-honed debate skills that I learned at Harvard, I have passionately delivered the "convince him he wants in" speech several times. And while you can convince a man to stick around for a few more months and play the part of the happy boyfriend, you can't convince that man to love and cherish you and be there for the long term. This is a decision that a man must come to on his own in his own time. In order to have a fully committed partner, you must give a man enough space to figure out what he wants on his own. Otherwise, you will likely find yourself in the same "confused boyfriend" situation soon after—or worse, having to deliver the same "We can do this, I promise" speech to him a few days before the wedding!

Never rationalize a man's reasons for telling you he doesn't know what he wants. Get to know yourself, what you want for your life, and what you want out of a relationship. You'll be able to spot genuine lifelong compatibility when you have it and be willing to gracefully bow out when you don't.

SELF-LOVE PRINCIPLE #12
**When a guy expresses doubt or hesitation
about being in an exclusive relationship with you,
this is not the time to step up and fill in the blanks for him.
You are responsible for writing your own life story—
not someone else's.**

If you chose C, you are a Dating Diva, a woman who knows how to date with dignity and without fear. This is who I want all women— including myself—to be. The Dating Diva knows that *men do not do anything they do not want to do.* I don't use the word "diva" to mean that you make dating you a difficult, frustrating task. It just means that you love yourself enough to know that you don't have to beg somebody to have a meaningful and fulfilling relationship with you.

When a man says that he doesn't know what he wants, the best thing you can do is give him space and move on with your life. Men are often slower than women at processing experiences and emotions. A man can easily coast in a relationship for years, taking the path of least resistance and never speaking up about his unhappiness, and then *poof!* one day he wakes up from his lazy haze to realize he is completely miserable and wants out. When a man expresses his uncertainty about being in a relationship with you, give him ample space and time to reflect. Don't try to help him think it through. Don't try to "be there" for him. Give him time to miss you. Men fall in love with women when they long for them— not when they are persuaded or guilt-tripped into being with them.

BYOB BROSPECTIVE

I asked one 28-year-old entrepreneur from Atlanta, GA what his ideal response would be from a woman if he told her he didn't know what he wanted. This is how he responded:

In a perfect world, she would say, "You know what? I understand where you're coming from. Go do you. Go find yourself. I'm going to do me." And I'm always happy when a woman tells me that. She may not be there when I get back, which is good because I don't want to be the person holding her up from having children. That would be the perfect scenario: I'll do my own thing, she'll do her own thing. And if I feel like she's the one for me, and she's still available, then let's give it another shot.

I know taking a big step back isn't easy to do. It's painful, frustrating, and especially hard for women who are accustomed to proactively solving problems at home, school, and work. No matter how much of a go-getter you are in other areas of your life, when a man tells you he isn't sure if he wants to be in a relationship with you, back off. Let whatever is supposed to happen play out naturally without your planning and plotting. Have the dignity to walk away from an unfulfilling, ambiguous situation. You owe it to yourself!

One important thing to keep in mind, though, is that giving a man space to think doesn't mean he'll come to the conclusion that he wants to be in a relationship with you. This is why you must truly move on when a guy tells you he doesn't know what he wants. By "moving on," I mean living a happy, single life and eventually dating other men. If he realizes he can't live without you, he'll come back. And then if there is still room in your life and in your heart, you can consider letting him back in.

Remember this: men persistently pursue what they want—especially when they know exactly what they are missing.

SELF-LOVE PRINCIPLE #13
Never chase after a man who says he doesn't know what he wants. Real men go after what they want.

A SELF-LOVE INSIGHT

My friend has a great saying that helps me keep things straight:
"If a man is interested in you, you'll know. If he's not, you'll be confused."

— 30 years old, New York City, NY, in a relationship

So there you have it. If a guy you are dating or flirting with constantly has you feeling confused, it's not because he's mysterious and complex; it's because he's just not that into you. I've read dozens of books that tell women how to date, detailing all kinds of rules, strategies, and tactics for making sure you catch and keep his attention. However, the one principle that has never steered me wrong is to be willing to let go of relationships that don't serve me. Part of that is stepping back from men who aren't sure they want to be with me. I love reading about men, relationships, love, and communication. However, rather than trying to remember tons of rules and exhaust myself with mental gymnastics in attempts to keep a guy, I focus on chasing my own joy—not any guy or relationship. This is the only thing I can control, and that will make me happier no matter what happens in the relationship.

Sometimes, after having time and space to think, your guy will conclude that he does not want the relationship after all. And while being rejected always hurts, it's part of the process of finding The One. Have the courage to face the reality of your incompatible desires and expectations—whether for the relationship or for life in general. Doing so frees you to find The One who genuinely wants the same things you want out of life. Letting go frees you to be with someone who wants to pursue his ideal life with you.

After ending a relationship, it's important that you not torture yourself with what you could have done differently or try to pinpoint the micromoment when things began to unravel. Be gentle, compassionate, and nurturing with yourself—just as you would treat your best friend if she were going through a painful breakup. I am the queen of Monday morning relationship quarterbacking. After a breakup, I am tempted to replay the entire relationship from day one, chastising myself for what I feel I should have done differently. While reflection is important, no amount of analysis will heal the broken relationship. I've learned that my first priority after ending a relationship should be to take care of myself, get centered again, and get back to creating a life that I love. It sucks when you want him to be your boyfriend and he's not ready. However, this is why you have friends, family, and books like this to help you heal your heart and be your own boyfriend.

The Power of Saying Goodbye

In the wake of a breakup, our minds' decision-making capabilities cannot always be fully trusted. We will bend ourselves into a warm salted pretzel, crafting rationalizations for why we should contact an ex-boyfriend and stay in touch. Here are some very good reasons not to stay friends with the vast majority of your ex-boyfriends, ex-lovers, and former hookup partners:

- You could end up hooking up, rekindling the fire of your attraction to him, and getting your heart broken—again.

- You could end up getting your feelings seriously hurt when he excitedly tells you about his new girlfriend—or worse, his fiancée.

- You could scare away guys who are interested in dating you but don't want to compete with a lingering ex-boyfriend.

- You put yourself in the position of never being able to completely get over him because you have constant reminders of him and how great things could be "one day."

- You may start to move on from the relationship only to learn that your ex wants to get back together with you! When you have to break the news to him that he's been moved into the "friend zone," you could end up hurting his feelings and then feeling guilty. Misplaced guilt or feeling like she "led him on" has driven many a woman into reentering a relationship she knew wasn't right for her. By having a clean break, you free yourself from any such feeling of relationship indebtedness.

- You could end up having bad-idea ex-sex with him, then get pregnant and still not end up together. Now, you're tied together for the rest of your lives—all because you wouldn't let the relationship go. It can happen, and it will be so much more difficult than letting go would have been.

- By refusing to say goodbye, you rob yourself of the opportunity to gain much-needed closure. If you constantly drag out the relationship, always looking for one last crumb, you never get the satisfying, peaceful feeling of ending one chapter so that you can begin another one.

KANEISHA CONFESSIONAL

When I moved back to Austin after the breakup with James, I created an online dating profile. Several months and many dates later, I was shocked to see that I had been matched with my high school sweetheart, Joshua. Twelve years after we had first met, our personalities were still complementary enough to make a dating website match us up. He looked great, and his profile reminded me of all the things I had loved about him in high school: his openness, his thirst for adventure, his love of nature, his creativity, and his deep connection to spirit. I fantasized about us reigniting our romance, falling back in love, getting married, and traveling the world together spreading love and light. I sent him a playful message to which he quickly and eagerly responded. He suggested we get together to reminisce and read our old love letters.

Rather than rushing to his house for a romantic reunion, I initially ignored his email out of fear of starting something again with him. I had just gotten out of a painful relationship, and I feared that Joshua and I would start a fire that we'd eventually have to put out. Feeling bad as well as curious about what could have been, I eventually called to apologize for ignoring his message and agreed to get together.

Over the next several weeks, we talked briefly a few times and played an awkward game of phone tag. It was obvious that we were both excited about the idea of seeing each other again, catching up on old times, and maybe even hooking up. However, we were both also very unsure as well. Our high school relationship had been passionate and tumultuous, full of lofty declarations of undying love punctuated by venomous arguments and attempts to control each another.

During this time while we played phone tag, I ran into Joshua at Barton Springs, a natural swimming hole in my neighborhood. We had a warm and friendly conversation. He sheepishly apologized for not calling me back. I told him I understood and we agreed that we didn't want to start anything up again. What we'd had in high school was special (though it was also unhealthy in ways). We didn't need to reminisce for hours together. We both knew our relationship had been more than just high school puppy love, and we wanted to keep it that way: special, memorable, and untainted by present-day drama. We talked about how we were each other's first loves, how we would always love one other, and then we hugged. I knew deep down that our goodbye hug was a meaningful one. The Universe had brought us back together one last time—not to reignite our relationship, but to say a proper goodbye. When I said goodbye to Josh that day, I felt like it would be the last time I would see him.

Less than three months later, I received a phone call from Josh's mom telling me that he had died in a car incident. I was devastated to hear that my high school sweetheart, my first love, someone who in some ways I considered my soulmate, was gone. I had lost family members before, but never had I lost someone whom I had loved the way I loved Joshua. I was in Oakland visiting my girlfriend Shadiah when I got the news. That night, I spent a long time in her backyard, bowing on my knees with my forehead pressed to the ground as I cried and processed the news. Despite the pain of mourning Joshua's death, I also felt a sense of peace.

In the wake of Joshua's passing, I was deeply grateful that we had been willing to let go of the romantic nature of our relationship and love each other from afar. By being willing to let go of someone that I deeply loved, I received the gifts of inner peace, closure, and the chance to say goodbye exactly how I wanted to.

No matter how tempting it is, how painful it may seem to never see or hear from your ex again, you gain more than you lose when you are willing to say goodbye to old relationships.

SELF-LOVE PRINCIPLE #14

**Letting someone go is an act of love for yourself
and for the other person.**

Part 2:
Unleash Your Sexy

Chapter 5:
Be Sexy for You

All women have a different sense of sexuality,
or sense of fun, or sense of what's sexy
or cool or tough.
— ANGELINA JOLIE

IN MIDDLE SCHOOL, I started to attract a lot of attention from the boys. Though I had never felt like an ugly duckling (some elementary school pictures might say otherwise), I had never thought of myself as a classic beauty. However, once boys started fighting over the privilege of carrying my books to class (yes, like in those old movies!), I began to think of myself as a very pretty girl. When boys pursued me and responded to my flirtatiousness, I reveled in the attention and came to believe that other people determined my beauty. In my mind, I was attractive and valuable because those boys thought I was pretty and showed me a lot of attention. That belief, which had seeped into my young subconscious, blocked me from cultivating an internally defined sense of self-worth and sexiness. For most of my life, I haven't had to try hard to get attention from men, so I eventually relaxed into a routine in which self-care was not a priority. I figured my time and energy were better spent focusing on other areas like getting into graduate school, succeeding in business, and hanging out with my friends.

As I near thirty, I'm finally growing into an authentic sense of womanhood. I'm learning that a woman's beauty comes from exuding grace, sexiness, calm, and confidence. Attracting attention from others is only a small part of the gift of femininity. Sexiness and sensuality are far more meaningful and complex than having a pretty face or a tight body (though of course that's nice too).

SELF-LOVE PRINCIPLE #15
**Sexiness is not a title bestowed upon you from others.
It's an attitude and lifestyle you claim for yourself.**

Kaneisha's Golden Dating Rule

Whereas the traditional golden rule is that you should treat others as you would want to be treated, Kaneisha's Golden Dating Rule is to treat yourself as you would want your partner to treat you. When you are single, it's easy to fall into the trap of pining after a boyfriend who doesn't exist.[4] Another trap is looking to the past

---

[4] Anyone else remember Jan's "boyfriend" George Glass from *The Brady Bunch Movie?*

and glorifying a guy that wasn't right for you. Like a well overflowing after many days of rain, it's natural for your love energy to build up during singlehood. Why not unleash that energy by befriending and romancing yourself? Go ahead, be your own boyfriend.

Below is a list of some romantic gestures I used to wish a man would do for me. When I realized that I could drink from my own well of love and happiness, I decided to do these things for myself.

Flowers. I come from several generations of women who are crazy about plants and flowers. We love to be surrounded by the vibrant energy and lush beauty of flora, and we take pride in our gardens and beautiful bouquets. I used to constantly drop hints and nag boyfriends to buy me flowers. Then I realized that I could buy a stunning bouquet for under $15 from Whole Foods and have fresh flowers whenever I wanted. I was surprised to learn that many men are excited to buy me "replenishment" flowers after seeing that I already buy them for myself. Rather than feeling like a whipped, sappy schmuck when he restocks my flower supply, the guy feels like he's doing something useful and manly—like taking out a twenty-pound bag of garbage—except he's bringing me a dozen pink peonies every week.

Great Dates. While I was in graduate school at Harvard, I wanted a man to whisk me around Boston, showing me the touristy sights and hole-in-the-wall treasures. I would daydream about all the charming places I would visit if only I had an adventurous boyfriend to accompany me. When I finally got sick of daydreaming, I decided to make time to explore the city by myself and with my friends. Sometimes, I would spend the day with a friend exploring the Boston Museum of Fine Arts. Other days, I would go have a picnic at Arnold Arboretum with my bestie Shadiah. Every week, I tried a new brunch spot with my girlfriends, and those regular brunch adventures became a cherished tradition. Some of my favorite memories are the afternoons I spent reading on a blanket by myself on the banks of the Charles River. If I had waited for a boyfriend to explore Boston with me, I would've missed out on all those delicious eateries, juicy girl talk, and luxurious afternoons lounging in nature.

Sexual Fulfillment. While our lesbian sisters have been fine without men for ages, many straight gals are still relying completely on men to fulfill their sexual cravings. I love a good sexfest with my lover like the next woman, but I don't have to be in a relationship to get my O on. With all that technology has to offer, why would any woman wait for a guy to give her an orgasm? Hot sex with a loving, committed partner is irreplaceable, but a good vibrator can help you out in the meantime (and make things even better with your boo once you have one).

The list of ways you can be your own boyfriend could go on forever: painting accent walls in your apartment, buying your first house, investing in grown-up furniture, going on a solo trip, learning how to drive a car with a manual transmission, etc. I do not mean to imply that most women depend on men for these things all the time. However, we have certain desires that often go unfulfilled because we're waiting for that big, strong man to swoop in and make the grand gesture. What most of us don't realize is that when you make the effort to be your own boyfriend, you often enjoy and appreciate the experiences more. You smile to yourself as you realize how wonderfully you are taking care of yourself. When you work out your self-love muscles by being your own boyfriend, you become better at recognizing a man who genuinely wants to be a great boyfriend to you. If you are a woman waiting around for a boyfriend to come along before you live your life the way you want to, you are wasting valuable opportunities to be your own hero.

SELF-LOVE PRINCIPLE #16

Don't wait for a man to come and give you something that you can give yourself.

Stop Depriving Yourself

Many of us grew up being told by our parents or our own nagging inner voice, "You *want* that. You don't *need* that," which led us to conclude that things you need are more important than things you want. So you learned to listen to your most basic needs like a growling stomach, a pounding migraine, or a damaged car engine. But when it comes to your wants (e.g., a beautifully decorated home, a sporty hybrid car, an exotic island vacation, or a fabulous and fulfilling job), you've developed a habit of neglecting them.

First, I'll make sure I have what I need to get by, you tell yourself, *and if there is any time, energy, and money left over, only then will I go after the things I want*. However, you never seem to get past taking care of your endless list of "needs" to the point where you can focus on your wants. Something always comes up and pushes your wants to the bottom of the to-do list. This happens because you attract what you pay the most attention to. If you're always focusing on putting out fires, you'll attract more fires.

SELF-LOVE PRINCIPLE #17
Focus your energy on vividly feeling how you would feel when you have what you want most and you'll get it.

If you focus on the thoughts, pursuits, and activities that bring you bliss and make life truly worth living, you'll inherently attract more experiences that make you say, "Yes, this is what I want. Thank you, and more please!"

Many of us deprive ourselves of the very things that could bring us the most happiness. It's almost as if we believe there is a limited quantity of goodness available to us, and we don't want to use it up for fear that one day, our goodness tank will sink to E, leaving us stranded in the middle of Miseryland. To the contrary, the more goodness fuel you use, the more sources you will find to fill it up. Some activities that bring me joy but are often abandoned in the name of everyday "maintenance" are cooking for myself, keeping my apartment clean, taking myself to the movies, giving myself luxurious at-home hair treatments, keeping a consistent fitness schedule, riding my bike, learning and practicing French, and journaling.

KANEISHA CONFESSIONAL

When I moved to Los Angeles after graduate school, I refused to buy a car, citing all the obligations and headaches that come with it. "I don't need a car," I told myself. "I work from home, live close to friends, and can walk to a plethora of stores and the beach." I had convinced myself I was happier without a car. My wake-up call came one day when I was at a restaurant and ran into Reverend Michael Beckwith, the founder of the world-renowned Agape International Spiritual Center and a featured expert in the best-selling book and documentary The Secret. *He asked me how long I'd been attending Agape services. I proudly replied, "Since 2005 when I was in college!" I didn't mention that in the last year, I'd only attended the center sporadically. In the six months I had lived in the area, I'd probably been to church five times. At that moment, I remembered how important being near my spiritual community had been in my decision to move to Los Angeles. I had yearned to be with people who shared my thirst for living a joyful, spirit-filled life, and I had found those people at Agape. However, getting there through public transportation wasn't easy. I ended up staying home most Sunday mornings and skipping the long and early bus ride to Agape.*

That was my breaking point. I realized I was sabotaging myself. Being an active member of a spiritual community was very important to me, but I was consistently isolating myself.

I never did buy a car while I lived in Los Angeles, but I learned two important lessons there: 1) Don't deprive yourself of what you need or want; and 2) Don't deceive yourself into thinking that you don't want something just because you aren't sure how you'll get it. It's better to be honest with yourself about what you really want— even if you aren't sure how to get it—than to pretend that you don't want it in the first place. When you pretend, you slam the door shut on ever getting what you want.

Our wants matter just as much as—if not more than—our needs. Our wants are what make us different from the next person. Every person has to eat, sleep, and seek shelter. But only you have your particular set of gifts, strengths, talents, wishes, preferences, hopes, and dreams. Your desires are what make you you. So although you won't physically die if you deprive yourself of your wants, you could slowly blow out your inner light.

SELF-LOVE PRINCIPLE #18
**Honor your wants as much as your needs.
Ignoring the desires that make you unique
is self-sabotaging and serves no one.**

So just do it: follow your bliss. Eat the food that makes your body sing with joy. Read the books that fill your heart with inspiration, compassion, and excitement. Spend time with the people who make you feel loved, energized, accepted, inspired, and understood. Seek out the experiences that warm your heart when you remember them. It's not selfish or indulgent; it's necessary.

KANEISHA CONFESSIONAL

As a writer, coach, and entrepreneur, I have the option of working from a home office, which is exactly what I did for the first three years of my career. As an entrepreneur, I didn't particularly enjoy working by myself at home all day, and from the first time I heard about coworking spaces, I knew it was exactly what I needed to be more productive and focused throughout my workday. However, I couldn't bring myself to pay several hundred dollars every month to work in a beautiful space with other people knowing I could work at home or in a coffee shop for free. The problem with that rationale was that I rarely actually got dressed and left the house to work at a coffee shop. I knew I'd be happy I'd gone once I got there, but since no one was really expecting me and I had a habit of working from home, it was hard to make myself go.

Over time, I admitted that I was wilting working from home, and I knew I had to do something. Finally, I threw in the towel and decided that I no longer had the "choice" of whether or not to cowork. It was something I actually needed to be a better writer and entrepreneur. From the first day I spent at a coworking space, I knew I was home. I landed two speaking engagements that day from businesswomen who were visiting the center, and I even made a new friend. I gave myself what I really wanted, and it worked out well for me.

Give yourself what you really want and don't apologize for it. You'll notice that once you begin to give yourself the things you want, more of your desires will be fulfilled. Your best life and highest self is waiting for you around the corner. Go find her!

Crazy Girls Anonymous:
Five Ways to Be Less Needy and Controlling

Contrary to what romantic comedies will tell you, one of the biggest turn-ons to a guy is a confident, happy, independent woman. However, even those of us who think of ourselves as fabulous, accomplished women can act needy and clingy in relationships *especially* after a prolonged period of neglecting ourselves and not being our own boyfriends.

BYOB BROSPECTIVE

Below, a 43-year-old network engineer from Rochester, NY describes his insecure ex-wife. She expected him to be there twenty-four hours a day, lifting her spirits and handling *everything* from travel to finances. The relationship, he says, was "mentally exhausting."

When you have to go away on business or you're consumed with another family problem, and you're not there to give them that attention all the time, overly needy women start folding. They don't understand what's wrong. It just spirals out of control.

He felt forced to decide whether to live his life or handle her needs.

It was a constant choice, which always brings a lot of stress.

Stress-inducing ladies seemed to be a common theme in my conversations with guys. I talked with a 28-year-old entrepreneur from Atlanta, GA, who told me that one of the quickest ways a girl can end a relationship with him is by stressing him out.

Just continuously calling me over and over will stress me out. If I don't pick up my phone the first time and she asks me a million questions about why I didn't pick up my phone, that will stress me out.

Here are some tactics to use when you think that you are being too needy with the man in your life:

1. Treat calling your boyfriend like eating candy.
I've said it a million times, and I'll say it again: straight men do not like talking on the phone as much as women do.   Rather than picking up the phone and calling your boyfriend several times a day or whenever you randomly feel like it, consider calling your boyfriend a decadent treat—something to be indulged in every once in awhile. Give him plenty of time to miss you. When you let your boyfriend be the one to call you, you are sure to have his full attention. The next time you get a nagging feeling to call your boyfriend, treat it like a candy craving. Ask yourself, "Is there a healthier substitute to satisfy this craving?"

2. Call a girlfriend, an aunt, good ole grandma, or some other friend who likes talking on the phone.
Sometimes we call our boyfriends just to gab, and that is a complete waste of your boyfriend-calling credits. You will come off as needy and erode the mystique that drew him to you in the first place. Most likely, you'll end up trying to keep him on the phone longer than he wants to be. If you simply must talk to someone, call a close friend and pour your heart out. Or even better . . .

3. Journal.

The best person to help you solve your problems is often yourself in partnership with your Source. Rather than running to your friends, parents, or boyfriend whenever you have a problem, take time to journal about it and reflect upon the situation. Is there something you can do right now to fix the problem? Is it really even a problem at all? Light a candle, put on some soothing Brazilian music, and start journaling away! You'll get all your feelings out on paper rather than burdening someone else with your anxieties. And of course, you'll also feel much better.

4. Don't call your guy when you are "running on empty."

The men in our lives want to be there for us when we are in need of support. Unfortunately, the way most men want to be there for us is to "fix" the problem rather than listen. This results in the two of you getting frustrated with each other. You don't think he's listening, and he thinks you're just whining. Rather than turning to your guy when you are absolutely drained of energy, take the time and space to rejuvenate yourself. Take a luxurious bath, read a magazine, and just relax. Men are more than happy to give us the space we need when we are stressed or tired. The problem is that we often look to our partners to infuse us with energy through their love and attention. It is not your guy's job to keep you happy and fulfilled. That's your job.

5. Don't fish for compliments and reassurance.

I used to have the very bad habit of fishing for compliments from my boyfriends. Sure, it feels comforting to have your boyfriend say wonderful things about you every single day. But those sweet messages are more meaningful when he is genuinely moved to say them. Fishing for compliments may seem all in good fun to you, but it makes you come off as needy and bossy. Don't do it!

SELF-LOVE PRINCIPLE #19
Neediness comes from a belief that the answers to your problems lie within other people. You have the answers to all your problems.

Stop Analyzing His Texts and Start Living Your Life: Keep It Moving and Expect Nothing

Harvard Business School is exactly where I belonged in my mid-twenties because I was obsessed with analyzing and solving problems. The caveat is that Harvard encourages us to apply analytical rigor to leadership challenges and business decisions, and I was intrigued with analyzing life, love, and relationship issues. While I'm happy to have an MBA to help me analyze business issues, I have learned that many circumstances of my dating life are simply not worth analyzing in detail. For example, in the past, nothing burned me up more than a guy not calling me after he specifically stated that he would. On those occasions, I refused to accept the possibilities that he might've forgotten or become busy. I put on my Ms. Smart Girl hat and indulged in inventing theories like these:

- *He's testing the boundaries of the relationship to see if I will tolerate his failure to follow through on his promises.*

- *He feels himself getting too close to me. He's trying to pull away and establish his independence.*

And then, as my worries spiraled out of control, I would eventually settle on:

Crap. He's just not that into me.

Even when I came to that conclusion, I often wasn't satisfied with merely accepting the awful truth. Rather, I felt compelled to analyze exactly what went wrong, when things began to unravel, and what I could do differently next time. Once in awhile, performing a multilevel analysis of why a guy and I didn't mesh gave me a temporary sense of control. But it never made me any happier.

Your conjecturing about a guy's undesirable behavior does not make him change. It wastes your time and mental energy, and even worse, saps your happiness and peace of mind.

Therefore, when you are dating a guy and he does something you do not appreciate or understand (particularly in the early stages of dating), just keep it moving. By "keep it moving," I mean go about your life, doing whatever you were doing before you met Mr. Inconsistent. As hard as it is to clear your mind, try your best not to worry about why he suddenly seems to have lost interest. The best thing you can do for yourself and the situation is to keep it moving. Do not bog yourself down with trying to figure out how to "set him straight." As Sherry Argov, author of *Why Men Love Bitches*, says, "Men do not respond to words. They respond to no contact." If you really want a guy to understand that you are unhappy with his behavior, deny him your company and attention. By setting boundaries on how you allow others to treat you, you protect yourself and show guys that you aren't so desperate that you'll take whatever crumbs of attention he throws your way. It's not about being difficult; it's about having standards.

Keeping it moving is not a call to play games or be passive aggressive. It's about taking a step back, relaxing, and focusing on doing what makes you happy. Otherwise, you'll end up focusing on the cause and origin of something that is making you unhappy. If you really want Mr. Maybe Right to stop making last-minute plans with you, don't go out with him when he tries to make these last-minute plans with you. If you want him to call you when he says he will, do not text him subtle reminders like, "Hope you're having a great day!" (Guys see right through those "just saying hi" texts, by the way.) Just keep it moving, have your own great day, and if he calls, great. If not, you will not have wasted time and energy on obsessing over it. It's all about subtly showing the man (or any person in your life for that matter) how you will allow yourself to be treated.

An important part of keeping it moving is to expect nothing. As an optimistic person with high expectations for myself and others, this has been a hard pill to swallow. But I have finally swallowed it, and I hope the timed-release capsule works well enough to continually remind me to expect nothing from guys I am casually dating.

By no means am I telling you to let people treat you badly. Simply put, you can't put expectations on people who have not earned the title associated with such expectations. "Expect nothing" is a reminder to let relationships develop at a natural pace rather than trying to accelerate them to the "next level" by increasing your expectations.

For example, if a guy is not your boyfriend, do not expect him to perform boyfriend duties like buy you romantic gifts, help you move out of your apartment, or go grocery shopping with you. If he does these things, awesome! He is likely doing these things because he wants to be your boyfriend. However, if you don't explicitly have that level of commitment from someone, yet you *expect* him to do these favors for you, you'll most likely end up disappointed and frustrated, and he will most likely end up confused and distant. Even if a man who is not yet your boyfriend is willing to do boyfriend activities with you, it's often a good idea to engage in such activities in moderation and for a limited period of time (e.g., three months). I have gotten myself very mixed up in the head because I spent a lot of time doing "boyfriend" things with men who weren't exclusively dating me or explicitly committed to me. Each time I spent a lot of time doing boyfriend-girlfriend activities with a guy who wasn't actually my boyfriend, I made him my boyfriend in my heart and mind, while in his mind, we were still casually dating, which included the option to date other people. This mismatch between your perceptions and reality is a recipe for disappointment that you can avoid if you—say it with me now!— expect nothing and keep it moving.

I have often been surprised at the devastation I feel when things end with someone I have been dating for just a short period of time. I think this disappointment comes from the fact that I build up a fantasy relationship of what could be in my mind. Often, I've introduced the guy to my friends and family, considered in detail what a future with him would look like, and have become very emotionally attached. When I'm in the worst stages of fantasizing, I've even started to consider changing life plans or even moving for the guy—all before he is even my serious boyfriend! When you start dating someone new, a little bit of fantasizing is fun and completely natural. How could I possibly tell a woman to not get her hopes up when she meets someone she's really excited about? Just don't get carried away to the point where your fantasy blinds you from reality.

When men and women have these misunderstandings, it's not always because either party is doing something wrong. As John Gray says in the classic relationship guide *Men Are from Mars, Women Are from Venus*, men and women often speak different languages even when we are using the same words. Men and women can easily run into misunderstandings due to our different communication styles. "Expect nothing and keep it moving" is one way that you can make sure you and your guy are at least speaking similar dialects while dating! The key is to keep your eyes wide open about the relationship that you are actually in—not the one you've created in your mind. Keeping it moving and expecting nothing is a way to maintain some balance in those early days of dating so that your feelings don't outpace the commitment you have in reality.

By following this mantra, you stay busy enjoying your life and being your own boyfriend. This is not about pretending not to care. Of course you care! You are simply making sure that your emotional investment stays in line with the natural development of the relationship rather than racing far ahead of it. Go on and live your life. Stop fretting over every text, instant message, and emoticon he sends—or doesn't send. Don't we have enough to keep us occupied without checking our call history every five minutes?

Now, "keep it moving" and "expect nothing" have to go together. Doing one without the other will not serve you. If you simply keep it moving yet consistently have boyfriend expectations from men you are casually dating, you will end up bouncing from one guy to the next, continually disappointed that reality doesn't live up to your fantasies. If you expect nothing without also keeping it moving, you will end up accepting crumbs in your dating life. You'll spend months or years dating men that you expect nothing from, and sadly, you will get just that: nothing.

The "Expect Nothing and Keep It Moving" method is most helpful in the early stages of dating and friendship. Rather than deciding how much the guy *should* care or how he *should* act, allow his words and actions to show you the quality of his character and his intentions. When you don't burden a relationship with expectations, you allow it to evolve naturally into what it is ultimately supposed to be.

BYOB BROSPECTIVE

One tendency that people have when they get into a relationship is that they lose themselves in the other person. So I think that if you want to be able to keep it moving, you have to keep your goals focused. For example, if you want to be an entrepreneur, that goal should never be negatively affected by your relationship status. And that doesn't mean that you have to be selfish. But it does mean that you're staying focused on being the best you that you can be.

— Lincoln Anthony Blades, author of *The Myth of the Multiple Orgasm*, blogger at ThisIsYourConscience.com

I'm still learning how to expect nothing and keep it moving, but I get better at it every day. The guys I casually date no longer have to hear my heated, hands-on-hips "I'm a catch who deserves to be treated with respect!" lecture. My friends don't have to listen to me whine, "Why doesn't he just do what he says he's going to do?!" And I have more time and energy to write, work on my business, hang out with my friends, date the guys who are most interested in me, and of course, date myself.

SELF-LOVE PRINCIPLE #20
**Once you start treating yourself really well,
you won't accept anything less from others.**

Chapter 6:
Claim Your Sexy

*We are all born sexual creatures, thank God,
but it's a pity so many people despise and crush
this natural gift.*
— MARILYN MONROE

OTHER WOMEN MAY BE SEXY, but that's just not me. Are you thinking this? I definitely did for a long time. I once thought that some women were simply born sexy and the rest of us were doomed to stand on the sidelines, admiring their sexy swag in bewildered awe. This is simply not true. Every woman—no matter her age, ethnicity, or dress size—has the ability to be sexy.

Claiming your sexiness requires a willingness to banish your self-defeating thoughts and to confidently claim it. You don't have to do anything to earn your badge of sexiness. Sexiness is your divine right!

Below are some common ways we discourage our own sexiness. I counter each one with my "no excuses, you can do it, girl" responses:

1. *I'm too young/old to be sexy.*
Once you hit the age of eighteen, you have my official permission to step into your sexiness and own it for the rest of your life. Whether you are twenty-one or sixty-one, sexiness is your birthright and should not be squandered!

2. *I don't have extra time to spend trying to be sexy.*
Rather than thinking of sexiness as a huge project you have to undertake, make it an everyday part of your life. Think of sexiness as a journey instead of a destination. You walk in your sexiness every single day, getting closer to showing the world the luscious goddess you are.

3. *I don't feel sexy, and people don't ever describe me as sexy, so how could I possibly even begin to be sexy?*
The first step to feeling sexy is taking time to concentrate on you. Focus on cultivating a private and personal sense of sexiness and determining what that means for you. Other people's reactions to your outer appearance are secondary to your own opinion of how the way you dress, speak, move, and behave makes you feel. People can certainly appreciate your sexiness, but they do not define it. You do.

4. *I could never look like the jaw-dropping gorgeous women on TV or act like a sleepy-eyed seductress, so why should I even try?*
One of the worst things you can do in your quest to unleash your

sexy is to compare yourself to other women. Sexiness is the domain of each individual, and you must concentrate on bringing out your best sexy self rather than comparing yourself to your neighbor who could be Kerry Washington's twin.

BYOB BROSPECTIVES

A lot of women that I've been with have had body issues or hang-ups about things like that. That just gets in the way of being relaxed and enjoying yourself.

— 28 years old, Los Angeles, CA, dating

The majority of women are sexy in their own way, but whether they choose to exude it or not is another thing.

— 31 years old, Washington, DC, single

I'll Have What She's Having: An Orgasm a Day

Every woman deserves the joy of a daily orgasm. And I'm not just talking about the kind that men with good stamina give. I'm talking about the excruciating buildup of anticipation and the exultant release that results from working hard at something you truly love. I call this feeling an experiential orgasm. And of course, I'm also talking about the importance of having a good ole physical orgasm everyday as well.

SELF-LOVE PRINCIPLE #21
**Give yourself one experiential orgasm
and one physical orgasm a day.
Yes, every single day.**

BYOB EXPERT ADVICE

Orgasms are essential! Women are their most powerful when they are tapped into their sexuality, and that involves daily pleasure. Orgasms release so much stress and tension and activate all of our senses all around our body. If it's done right, an orgasm makes us very acute, very aware, and very productive.

— Arielle Loren, sexuality writer, documentary
filmmaker, founder of *CORSET* magazine

Don't let your life get so busy that you don't have enough time to give yourself the daily pleasure of an experiential orgasm. One quick activity can be the difference between a mediocre or stressful day and a delightful, memorable day.

Here are some examples of experiential orgasms:

- Painting a picture and then prominently displaying it in your home office

- Cooking a fantastic meal and then savoring every morsel over candlelight

- Laughing so hard with your friends that your stomach hurts and your eyes water

- Enjoying a scenic morning run by the river and then drinking freshly squeezed lemonade

As for achieving the physical orgasm, girl, just get yourself a great vibrator!

Why? you ask:

- Because you may be single and not interested in engaging with strange men's penises.

- Because your guy might be tired, busy, or out of town.

- Because your man might not be working it just right that night. (For the record: I do not recommend whipping out a sex toy after having sex with your boyfriend. Get yourself a waterproof model you can use privately in the bathtub while he's glued to the couch watching ESPN.)

A SELF-LOVE INSIGHT

Don't forget to be your own boyfriend in the bedroom. Self-pleasure can be a wonderful way to reconnect with yourself the same way sex can help you reconnect with a person. It's becoming intimate with yourself—and with no one to judge you. As long as it makes you feel good and there are no dead animals involved, go for it!

— 28 years old, Austin, TX, in a relationship

Sex toy shops have come a long way from the fluorescent-lit hovels you might imagine are crawling with creeps and perverts. Use an online review site like Yelp to find a tasteful shop where knowledgeable employees can help you. If you are too embarrassed to walk into a novelty shop, you can find something that tickles your fancy online. Vibrators are so widely available, you can even peruse reviews and then buy one online at Amazon!

KANEISHA CONFESSIONAL

I was reluctant to buy a vibrator, so one of my girlfriends bought one for me as a birthday surprise. She filled it with batteries and left it on my bed in my college dorm room. That tactic was surprisingly effective at getting me to use it. I passed on the gift (the gesture— not my vibrator) by buying one for a friend and doing the same thing.

Another way to experience orgasms regularly could be to consider practicing Orgasmic Meditation, which is also referred to as "OMing." I first learned about this practice after seeing Nicole Daedone, founder of the organization OneTaste, speak about the practice. In short, OMing involves a woman lying naked from the waist down, legs butterflied open while a male partner strokes the upper left part of her clitoris—the one o'clock position if her clitoris were a clock—for fifteen minutes. The woman experiences a profound physical orgasm, and the experience is meaningful and pleasurable for the man as well!

There is much more to OMing than I have explained here, and I have yet to try it. But from what I've seen and learned about

Orgasmic Meditation, it is the real deal and every orgasm-loving woman (including me!) should give it a try.

Let's start an "orgasm a day" revolution! Think about how much better the world would be if women had a physical and experiential orgasm a day:

1. We would be in better physical shape.
The physical exertion often required to climax—especially with an energetic partner—burns calories while releasing delicious endorphins.

2. We would be in better spiritual shape.
When you feed your spirit with sensual, delightful experiences, you are more present, grateful, balanced, and relaxed.

3. We would know ourselves better.
By exploring what pleasures our bodies, minds, and spirits, we slowly start to build a catalog of knowledge about what makes us satisfied and fulfilled. Daily orgasms help us maintain perspective about what matters most to us in life and encourage us to make self-pleasure and self-love a fundamental part of our daily routine.

Just What the Love Doctor Ordered: How to Get Your Daily Double Dose of Orgasmic Pleasure

Even if you know getting your daily O is ultra-important, you may not be exactly sure how to get the job done. No, this isn't about to be a sex lesson from Kaneisha. It's just two quick tips to help you consistently pleasure your body and your soul.

Acknowledge what makes you happy and do it.

We all have different notions of what is fun. No matter how wacky, seemingly boring, or unusual your interests and hobbies are, they are important if they make you happy. Don't put them on the backburner just because your hobbies and interests don't fall into popular categories of "fun." For example, I'll be thirty years old soon, and I still *love* a sleepover with my girlfriends and gay boys. Lots of people might roll their eyes and think "weirdo . . ." But for me and my friends, cooking an elaborate meal together, telling funny stories for hours, and using YouTube videos to learn the latest line dance before flopping onto air mattresses is still a ton of fun.

It often takes a conscious effort to remember and honor what makes you happy. The more often you practice doing what makes you happy, the more you will naturally turn to your happiness triggers when faced with boredom, sadness, or other feelings that might otherwise prompt you to look for solace or entertainment in a man.

Schedule time into your day for your daily orgasms.

When it's bedtime, don't just nod off to sleep after checking your email one last time. Once you finish your nightly beauty routine, give yourself some sexual healing before drifting off into dreamland. Integrating orgasm time into your nightly routine makes having your daily physical orgasm as natural as brushing your teeth!

As for experiential orgasms, schedule time into your day to do the activities that bring you these small but essential doses of happiness. While many experiential orgasms may require planning, you can easily sneak in a quickie. The next time you feel like zoning out on Facebook or Twitter for twenty minutes, tear yourself away from the computer and give yourself your experiential or physical orgasm for the day. Go ahead, take a fifteen-minute walk or light some incense and watch the smoke curl up in the air.

Green Lights Are Sexy

One of the quickest ways to up your sexiness factor is to radiate happiness. However, even the most optimistic, cheerful person gets in an inexplicable funk every now and then. If you find yourself feeling down, don't dwell in the blues overanalyzing your emotions. Remember that this mood can pass quite quickly if you distract yourself with a helping of happiness candy.

Long ago while browsing motivational YouTube videos (am I the only person who does that?), I stumbled upon a simple concept of green lights and red lights throughout one's day.[5] The love-your-work guru in the video spoke about the necessity of getting more green lights in your day to move toward living your best life. Every day, every hour, we are engaged in activities that are either green lights or red lights for us.

Green-light activities energize you and make you feel strong. You don't necessarily have to be skilled at these activities. They simply make you feel joyful, uplifted, and often challenged. Conversely, red-light activities make you feel drained, tired, and weak. You are relieved when they are over. The catch is that you may be very skilled at doing things that are actually draining red-light activities for you.

The motivational speaker in the video proposed that for a few days, you keep track of each hour of your day and note whether you are spending your time doing green-light or red-light activities. At the end of several days, you'll see not only how you spend your time but also which activities are energizing or draining. Even if you don't take the time to log your activities throughout the day, it's helpful to step back every once in awhile and check in with yourself and ask, "Is this a red-light or a green-light activity? Do I have to be doing this? Did I voluntarily sign up for this, and if so, how can I make sure I do or don't do this again? Is there a way to turn this red-light activity into a green-light activity?"

Of course, there are responsibilities in life that may be red lights but have to get done such as paying bills, washing dishes, etc. However, there are ways to lessen the burden of red-light activities to make them ever so slightly more enjoyable. For example, driving

---

[5] Although I can't remember the name of the motivational speaker in this particular video, his message has stayed with me and boosted my mood many times.

in traffic is a red-light activity (literally) for most people. Make a fabulous playlist of your favorite songs or download a few juicy audiobooks or podcasts to listen to in your car to make that stop-and-go drive at least a yellow-light activity.

When I have too many red-light activities in my day, it takes a physical and emotional toll on me. I feel exhausted, tense, and get neck pains. I even start to feel resentful of those responsibilities, even if I know they must be done to enable me to do the other things in my life that I enjoy. During those times, when I stop and think about how I got myself in such a red hot mess, I realize that I actually volunteered for the red-light activity. This is the result of not saying "no" enough, but also of not having a clear distinction between things I do well and things I actually enjoy doing. I mistake competencies as my strengths. However, as the speaker in the YouTube video said, if a skill or activity makes us feel weak—even if we are very good at it—it's more of a weakness than a strength.

Give yourself the gift of many green lights—like orgasms—throughout your day. Don't treat them as secondary to all the red-light stuff you have to do. The red-light obligations will always be there. Get enough green lights in your day, week, month, and life to make all the red lights a little less glaring.

Here are a few ideas for quick and easy green-light activities to light up your life:

1. Do something nice for yourself.
Whether it's buying yourself a pretty scarf, cooking hummus from scratch and leisurely savoring it, or giving yourself a manicure, taking the time to do something nice for yourself is a great way to

add more green lights to your day. I'm always pleasantly surprised by how much happier I feel when my nails are shaped and painted nicely. I feel more calm, more put together, and more able to take on the day. Perhaps it's because I'm a writer and see my hands while I type all day. Even though it's a little thing, a great manicure is a constant reminder that I took the time to make myself feel beautiful in a small but meaningful way.

2. Do something nice for someone anonymously.

Being someone's fairy godmother is the perfect way to remind yourself of life's many simple joys. Leave a coworker a nice note of appreciation. If a waiter or waitress treats you well, tell the restaurant manager. Nominate someone you know for an award without claiming credit. You'll be repaid for your kindness with an immediate and lasting boost to your mood.

3. Play a dance song and jam out like no one is watching.

Whether you're a smokin' hot dance diva or you are rhythmically challenged like me, dancing is an excellent way to exercise and have fun. My favorite station on Pandora for getting my no-shame-in-my-game dance on is the "Girlicious" station.

4. Smell a lemon.

I swear by the mood-enhancing abilities of the scent of citrus. Perhaps it's the combination of the shiny bright yellow peel, the juicy glimmer of the lemon flesh, and the alert aroma of lemon zest, but I can't think of a happier smell than that of a lemon. If lemons don't do it for you, try sniffing vanilla, jasmine, or fresh linen.

5. Just smile.
If you're not feeling happy, trick your mind into thinking you are. Simply smiling will activate the feel-good chemicals that make us happy. Before you know it, your fake smile will turn into a real one.[6]

Those were just some of my go-to personal favorites. Yours could be going for a run, playing chess with your grandpa, napping in the sun, or like our reader below, vividly imagining yourself dressing up as every single member of the rock band Queen.

A SELF-LOVE STORY

"Serena" tells how she fantasized about dressing up as a Queen cover band and recording YouTube videos. The newly single 28-year-old from Austin plays drums, bass guitar, and sings. She says she listened to Queen while she was doing errands, imagining herself putting on a one-woman show.

I was driving around in my car, singing along to Queen and laughing because I was thinking about all the stupid things I could do dressed up like a Queen cover band. I just laughed at myself the whole time. I was just thinking, "This is just great! I can make myself laugh. I'm hilarious!"

---

[6] Now, this isn't meant to be a long-term coping strategy. If you find yourself feeling down very often, it's time to get to the source of your unhappiness. See Chapter 3 for tips on getting your happy back.

SELF-LOVE PRINCIPLE #22
Don't dwell in a temporary funk. Give yourself an instant dose of happy and go on about your day. A happy woman is a sexy woman.

Your Home Is Your Oasis

Whether you live alone, with your family, roommates, or a beau, your home should be an oasis. All too often, we treat our homes like a dumping ground—a place to dump our junk wherever it lands and a place to dump our weary bodies at the end of the day. Instead of treating your home like a trash heap or a bare-bones jail cell, take the time to make your home a beautiful, comfortable oasis, and then work to keep it that way.

KANEISHA CONFESSIONAL

The sexiest spot in my home is my balcony. It's large and sun-drenched with blooming flowers and a bistro table with four differently colored chairs that I painted with my mom. During the day, it's the perfect place for me to sit and write, read, or take phone calls. In the evenings, I turn on the outdoor string lights and it transforms into a romantic French café in my own home. I often have friends and family over to drink wine here in my sexy little slice of Europe.

Here are some tips for creating an oasis at home:

1. Keep the clutter out of your sexy sacred space.
Clutter in your physical surroundings will crowd your mind and your spirit. I don't care how much you hate cleaning; it's imperative that you make time to declutter your surroundings. This means that you actually throw things away or donate them immediately—not just move them from one place to another! Being sexy requires that you be fully present in both mind and body, and you can't be present when you are distracted by wrinkled receipts, unfolded laundry, piles of mail, and a broken lamp.

2. Create a sexy sleeping atmosphere.
Ever since college, I have made it a priority to make my bed a luxurious sleeping experience on a budget. I love my plush "hotel bed" and strongly believe everyone should have one. We've all heard the importance of getting your beauty sleep. When you give yourself the gift of a sexy sleeping atmosphere, it's like giving yourself a super boost of sexy every night.

3. Color yourself sexy.
When decorating your home, think purposefully about color and pattern. Whether you surround yourself with bright colors and lively patterns or calm, sensual tans and whites, decide what kind of feeling you want each of your rooms to have and use colors to help you achieve your desired mood.

4. Surround yourself with sexy scents.
From your shower gel to your perfume to your room fragrance, pleasant smells can drastically influence your mood. As I

mentioned before, I lemon-scented bath soaps, jasmine-scented perfume, and cotton-scented room fragrances. Surround yourself with beautiful scents inspired by nature all day to get your sexy on, using all five senses.

5. Let your sexy light shine.

Make sure that your oasis is flooded with natural light during the day and that you have lamps and candles that can set the mood in the evening. If you live somewhere that starves you of natural light during the winters, consider buying a full-spectrum lamp that simulates sunlight. My roommate at Harvard, Chai, had one, and her room always looked so deliciously bright. Owning a "sun light" is like having your own personal on-demand sunshine!

6. Hang up pictures.

Though I am terrible at printing and putting up photos, I know how great it makes me feel when I do. Hanging up photos reminds us of all the people who love us, great memories we've had, and moments of beauty that we have experienced. Think of great photos and art on your wall as orgasms for the eyes.

So look around your bedroom and your apartment. Do you feel like you've stepped into a little piece of heaven? You should!

Handcuffs, Whips, and Plugs, Oh My!: Girl, Go Ahead and Let Your Freak Flag Fly

We're all familiar with the mysterious notion of the little understood, but ever-exalted sexual freak. In Western culture, our collective obsession with "freaks" is especially evident in our most popular music. Rick James's eighties dance hit "Super Freak" dedicates an entire song to the "very kinky girl" in his life. Rapper Ludacris proclaims that he wants a "lady in the street but a freak in the bed." If you asked Missy Elliott for advice, she'd say, "Get ur freak on." Recently, the popularity of *Fifty Shades of Grey* has brought "kinky fuckery" to the masses. I'm here to jump on the bandwagon and encourage you to let your freak flag fly, girl!

By no means am I the queen of freakery. In fact, I suspect that I rate on the lower side of the "freak number" scale (I'm working my way up). But with each year that passes, I realize how much more interesting physical pleasure and intimacy—with or without a partner—can be. There's much more pleasurable experimentation you can do beyond reverse cowgirl, vibrating rabbits, and playing dress-up (although those are all very fun as well).

BYOB BROSPECTIVE

Men generally tend to want to push the envelope sexually a little bit more than women do. Finding a partner who is healthy and open about her sexuality is just nice.

— 28 years old, Los Angeles, CA, dating

Letting out your inner Super Freak requires a few simple things (cape and handcuffs optional):

- Get a fundamental education in the workings of the human body: "Oh, so *that's* where the G spot is?!"

- Have a willingness to learn about and enhance your knowledge of sexual positions and techniques. A night of watching instructional videos on YouTube can give you the twenty-first century sex ed course for grown-ups you always wanted.

- Try new things on your own and become aware of what you do and don't like: "Ooh, let's try that again!"

- Speak up confidently about your preferences: "Use your teeth, mothafucka!"

- Ask your partner what he likes and do the things that turn him on: "Okay, okay, I'll wear the leather chaps this one time . . ."

- Experiment, learn, and gently give each other candid feedback: "I love it when you go down on me, but could you slow down a little bit? This isn't the last five minutes of the Indian lunch buffet."

SELF-LOVE PRINCIPLE #23
Give yourself the gift of exploring your body and learning what gives you pleasure with and without a partner.

Being a "freak" does not mean you run around without standards for your sexual activities. In fact, freakery at its best is born out of a deep respect for the power of sexual intimacy and a commitment to exploring this power to its fullest without shame or guilt. The aspiring freak should never do anything that is outside of her spiritual values, moral compass, or common sense. For the majority of you who are law-abiding citizens, you should avoid getting your freak on in any way that involves illegal activities or anything that makes your inner "This ain't right!" alarms go off.

Fit, Flexible, and Fabulous: Strategies for a Sexy Body

Being a freak is no fun if you always get tired halfway through sex or feel self-conscious about how you look in your lingerie. Being fit and flexible will make sure that you feel fabulous while you get your sexy on. Here are some tips to get you started:

- Make some form of exercise a nonnegotiable part of your daily life. Whether it's nature walks, hot yoga, or belly dancing lessons, moving your body is essential to unleashing your sexy.

- Drink enough water. Keep that sexy body hydrated, girl!

- Eat foods with the highest amount of life-giving nutrients as possible. In other words, eat more fresh, unprocessed foods (organic fruits and vegetables) and avoid excessive animal products (meat, eggs, dairy, etc.).

- Practice proper posture. Ain't nothing sexy about a hunchback.

- Have a boudoir photo shoot with a professional photographer. Hint: Craigslist is **not** the place to find the photographer. Ask your close friends if they know anyone or work with someone who has a professional website and past clients you can speak to.

- Buy beautiful lingerie and wear it whether or not a man is around.

- Have regular bikini waxes even if you are the only person who will see your well coiffed cooch.

KANEISHA CONFESSIONAL

Years ago, I went to the aesthetician for a bikini wax because my long-distance boyfriend at the time was coming for a visit. When she asked me what look I wanted for my lady parts, I replied, "I'm not sure. I didn't ask my boyfriend what he likes." My aesthetician's reply was fantastic and spot-on with the BYOB philosophy. She said (in a sexy Eastern European accent no less), "Oh, we do not get bikini waxes for men's pleasure. It's for us to enjoy first. Being groomed makes us feel sexy and powerful. It's a gift to yourself." Her message

*left such a lasting impression on me, I've gone for bikini waxes
regularly ever since—whether or not anyone else appreciates them!*

- Keep your eyebrows groomed via threading or waxing.

- Give yourself luxurious at-home pedicures and manicures.

- Keep your lips moisturized and supple.

- Give your hair a deep conditioning.

- Get your hair cut in a flattering style that's easy for you to maintain on your own.

- Get rid of all raggedy underwear. I have a zero-tolerance policy for granny panties—no exceptions for "period panties."

- Get enough sleep, meaning at least seven hours per night.

- Sleep on a silk pillowcase to cut down on acne breakouts and to protect your hair from having all the moisture sucked out by highly absorbent cotton pillowcases.

- Wear facial moisturizer with sunscreen every day and use a hydrating serum if you have thirsty skin.

- Create a bag with travel-size versions of all of your beauty essentials so that you don't skimp on self-care and beauty routines while on the road.

- Remove chipped nail polish immediately rather than letting it chip off over time.

- Wear clothes that truly fit you no matter what size you are.

- Floss daily or as close to daily as you can muster.

- Find a sexy perfume and make it your signature scent.

- Go to a lingerie shop to discover your real bra size and commit to wearing bras that are the right size.

- Get regular massages. Try massage schools or sign up for a daily deals website to get discounts on all different types of massages.

- Consult a professional stylist to help enhance your sexy.

KANEISHA CONFESSIONAL

When I first started writing this book, I didn't feel qualified to give advice about sexiness. Though I knew that "Unleash Your Sexy" was an essential part of the Be Your Own Boyfriend *philosophy, I absolutely did not feel sexy. In fact, I didn't even feel that I really looked all that put together. I felt that my daily look was girlish, harried, and haphazard. While I was working on the "Unleash Your Sexy" part of this book, I didn't live in a sexy environment and enjoying sensual delights was not a priority for me. However, after attending the blogging conference Blogalicious, where I was surrounded by hundreds of beautiful, sexy women of all ages, I knew that I was finally ready to make the leap to the world of sexy. In fact, I hired a professional image consultant I met at the conference.*

During my initial consultation with Monica, she asked me lots of questions about my current style (or lack thereof), my goals, and what look I was going for. We settled on the idea that I would go for what Monica termed a "youthful deconstructed glam" look. The next day, I prepared for our two-hour in-person consultation by hauling all of my clothes out into the living room and laying them out in piles by type—tops, dresses, bottoms, jackets, etc. Monica had me try on my go-to outfits and amazed me when, using my own clothes and accessories, she showed me how to take my go-to outfits from "young and cute" to sophisticated and sexy.

Then came the hilarious part of the entire experience. We went through every item I owned and tossed it in the "wear" or "donate" piles. I felt like I was on a makeover show as I bashfully watched Monica inspect each item, frequently handing over some stained, pilling, ill-fitting piece for the donate pile.

After we finished going through my entire wardrobe, Monica had me look through the image consultant's version of inkblots: laminated pages from magazines featuring layouts of various looks. She had me point out which items I liked and didn't like so she could get a better idea of my preferences. This exercise helped Monica create my style guide: a list of ten essential items as well as a longer list of nice-to-haves once I had gotten my foundation pieces out of the way.

Since I had an important networking event in New York City to attend, she made me a quick list of the items I needed to create my youthful deconstructed glam look. The next day, I set out to the mall with my shopping guidelines, which included specific items I should buy as well as the green-light (good) and red-light (stay away!) stores. Throughout the entire experience, Monica was by my side (virtually via Twitter) as I tried on the peep toe heels, fitted blazer, elasticized belt with minimal metalwork, and other items on my shopping list. For the first time in years, I was calm, focused, and confident while shopping, rather than feeling overwhelmed, distracted, and discouraged.

At the end of my two-hour shopping expedition, I had all the items on my "youthful deconstructed glam" look list and had stayed within my budget. I felt wonderful getting dressed for the event and exuded sexiness, confidence, and polish in my outfit. Somehow by dressing differently than I usually did, I actually felt more like myself. The next day, I woke up and realized that I had made a quantum leap: I was now ready to own my sexiness. And the missing, impossible-to-write portion of this book was finally born.

Chapter 7: Go Out, Sexy!

*Life should not be a journey to the grave
with the intention of arriving safely in a pretty
and well preserved body, but rather to skid in
broadside in a cloud of smoke, thoroughly used up,
totally worn out, and loudly proclaiming,
"Wow! What a Ride!"*
— HUNTER S. THOMPSON

AN IMPORTANT PART of maintaining your sexy is going out, having fun and letting the world revel in your sexy. Being social in a way that works for you is very sexy. However, I recognize that regularly going out isn't easy for everyone.

Even though I am a very extroverted person, I go through phases of being a hermit. I sometimes find myself in an antisocial rut, and the thought of getting out of my pajamas and leaving my comfortable apartment seems so unappealing. When this happens, it's usually because I feel out of place, misunderstood in a new environment, or out of balance.

No matter what environment you find yourself in, there is always another person who is thinking, "I want to be having fun— just not the kind of fun everyone else seems to be having!" Your job as a social, sexy woman is to find the people who like your kind of fun and to have a great time doing what makes you happy.

"But what about those of us who are just introverts?" you may be asking. Don't worry, I haven't forgotten that not everyone is a super-extrovert like I am. I know that many people get their energy from having lots of quality alone time. This spectrum is not about replacing your quality alone time; it's about all that alone time you have when you'd rather be doing something fun with other people. It's important to know the difference between taking time to rejuvenate your spirit and cutting yourself off from the world. You are trapped in the cycle of being a hermit if . . .

1. You want to go out, but you always end up staying in.
Even though you want to go out, you get anxious at the thought of getting dressed up and having to hang out with people you do or don't know—so you stay in.

2. You stay in for the night, but you're not doing something you truly enjoy.
You're piddling around on the Internet, watching television without much interest, restlessly reorganizing your hair accessories, ironing clothes that you haven't worn in ages—basically passing the time. If someone called you to go out, you would jump at the chance, but there's no way you're going to make the first move.

3. You rarely commit to showing up.

You make a habit of responding to social invitations by saying, "I'll check if I'm available and get back to you." You know you're free, but you don't want to commit in case you get skittish the day of the event. This tactic often works to make sure you don't commit to anything you don't want to do, but sometimes it works too well, and you end up rarely going out—even when you want to.

While taking time to take care of yourself is always a good thing, being a hermit is no good because . . .

1. You can lose perspective.

Solitude is an important part of being comfortable with yourself and enjoying your own company. But if you spend that time ruminating over the areas of your life that aren't going well, you'll end up obsessing about them and making yourself even more unhappy.

2. You lose touch with your friends.

A huge part of friendship is spending time together in person (and no, playing Words with Friends online does not count), being vulnerable with one another, and helping one another through difficult times. If you are feeling sad or lonely, it's okay to reach out to a friend for some company. Everyone gets lonely, and you shouldn't compound the situation by isolating yourself. Your friends love you and they want to be there for you. Let them! By reaching out to your friends, you'll help reinforce your relationships and solve the loneliness problem at the same time.

3. It perpetuates the situation.

The less you go out and the more you stay in, the less accustomed you become to finding things you like to do and doing them. Staying home becomes the *de facto* decision, and the dissatisfaction you might have once felt about your hermit lifestyle becomes your normal state.

4. You miss out on learning from other people.

When you're isolated and accustomed to always doing things your way, you could become inflexible and closed-minded. This makes you boring—and there is nothing sexy about boring people!

You deserve to live a life full of laughter, excitement, and dreams fulfilled. Breaking out of the hermit life is not easy, but it can be done with practice. Go out and make some memories!

Here are some tips for breaking out of the hermit cave and joining the world:

1. Venture out for mundane tasks and errands.

If you usually work from home or a stuffy office, take your laptop and set up shop at a nearby coffee shop or local bookstore with free wifi. The simple act of being around people can lift your spirits and make you feel connected to the human race.

The next time you buy a meal, don't even think about slinking out of the restaurant with a paper bag full of takeout and then eating it while watching a rerun of *Girls*. Proudly eat alone in the restaurant. I've done both the slink-out lunch and the sophisticated solo dinner enough times to know that I feel much better when surrounded by people. I do not feel like a creepy loser when I eat by myself in public. In fact, I feel confident and womanly. Sometimes, friendly strangers will talk to me. One time, an anonymous person even paid for my lunch! Heeey! I often feel a sense of camaraderie with my fellow solo diners. Try it. I bet you will enjoy it more than you think.

2. Plan your social calendar ahead.
Don't wait until the end of the workweek to start thinking about your plans for Friday evening. Often people will already have made their plans (that apparently you are not included in) or will settle into their own hermit status by the time Friday evening rolls around. Reach out to friends to make plans for the weekend a few days in advance, especially if the things you like to do require advance planning.

3. Be flexible.
Hermits often perpetuate their loneliness by insisting on going somewhere nearby, arbitrarily avoiding certain venues, or being overly frugal. For example, don't be *that friend* that never wants to go to any club that has a cover charge—unless you are fine with not being invited out by your friends when they decide to dance away the night there without you. It's completely fine to have limits and be mindful of your spending, but make these boundaries your private guidelines you create for yourself. Don't treat them as social dealbreakers that you declare to your friends. Life is too short! Create your evening plans with your friends and try to compromise so that you all end up having a great night.

4. Be honest with yourself about what you like.
If the thought of getting sweaty backing it up on the dance floor

doesn't appeal to you, don't scare yourself out of making plans entirely. Going out doesn't exclusively translate to a wild night at the club. If you're a fan of theater, invite a friend to a play and have dessert afterward. If you are an avid video gamer, organize a coed video game tournament at your place complete with pizza and beer. If you love to cook, invite a small group of people over to sample your latest creation or even have them come early to help prepare the meal. Create your own version of whatever a great night is and then include people in those plans.

The next time you are debating whether or not to pick up the phone and make plans, just do it. Your spirit will thank you and your friends will be glad to hear from you.

Now, if you're thinking, "What friends?" you may have been holed up for too long. Don't worry, you're not alone. There are countless ways to make new friends.

What Does a Girl Have to Do to Get Some Friends Around Here?!: Places to Find Friends

If you're in search of new friends and you haven't discovered Meetup.com, it's time to get with it! The site allows you to join or create local groups that share your interests. I've seen all kinds of groups based on many different interests: from wine tasting to business networking to hiking to breast-feeding. (In fact, remember how I mentioned OMing earlier? There's a group for that!) Even if you already have plenty of friends, joining several activity-related groups through Meetup will alert you to a myriad of fun activities as close or as far as you'd like to go. Of course, Meetup isn't the only way to meet new people, but it's a great resource for finding like-minded locals.

Here are some ways to find friends for fun and learning:

1. Join Toastmasters, the softball team, or a workplace affinity group.
If the events are mediocre or there isn't a club that seems interesting to you, start one. One of my friends (who is now in a very happy relationship) met her boyfriend through playing on the same club soccer team.

2. Find a spiritual community that resonates with you.
It can be a traditional church, temple, synagogue, mosque, or simply a group of people who enjoy getting together and discussing spiritual issues. A group of people who have shared values will often find it easier to bond even when not talking about spiritual issues.

3. Join a professional organization or mastermind group for women.
Depending on your profession, you can meet not only friends but a business partner as well. Just be sure you understand the difference between a networking event and fun girl talk over margaritas. Not all women are receptive to making friends at professional networking events (though I surely am!).

4. Go regularly to fitness classes such as yoga, spinning, Zumba, or Pilates.

People are very open to chatting right before and right after those kinds of classes. In fact, I met one of my besties Carla when we were both falling all over ourselves in the back row of an intermediate-level aerobics class in college. Neither of us ever went back to that class, but we ended up living together, traveling together, and have now been friends for more than ten years!

5. Meet friends through other friends.

If you have a friend that you love to spend time with, tell her you are working on building up your friend bank and that you'd love to hang out with her and her friends the next time they hang out. Another way to meet new people is by asking your existing friends to match you up with new friends. Don't be afraid to go on a blind friend date! I've done it three times and every time, it was instant friend love. The connection may not always happen, but when it does, it can be magical.

Which One of Us Is Samantha? I Know I'm Carrie!: The Best Friends a Girl Could Ask For

My close friend Leah loves the quote, "You are the average of your five closest friends," because it reminds her of the importance of being mindful of the company she keeps. For many of us, our friends are our chosen family. We know one another's deepest hurts and hopes, look to one another for companionship and fun, influence one another's decisions, travel and vacation together, and even spend holidays together.

Our friends influence us through their words, actions, examples, and advice. Thus, our friends and our social lives have tremendous potential to hinder or help our success in living happy, fulfilled lives. I've learned over the last few years that I want more from my friends than simply hanging out and having fun. I seek friends that help me stay true to my passions, goals, and principles, and whom I can support in return.

Below are traits that all of my closest friends have in common:

- They support and encourage me in achieving my personal and professional goals; even if it's merely listening to my excitement about my latest book idea.

- They share their own victories and struggles. They make it clear that they want my help and support, and I am thrilled to give it.

- We have at least one strong common interest that we can engage in together, whether it's building our businesses, finishing our books, becoming more fit, or learning new spiritual practices.

- They share in the responsibility of maintaining the friendship. I don't have to do all the work of planning get-togethers or checking in.

- We intentionally set aside time to have fun together. We also enjoy sitting around and doing nothing together.

- After spending time with them, I feel happy, inspired, and encouraged.

- They help me focus on being positive and proactive rather than feeding my sense of self-pity or martyrdom during difficult times.

- They gently and lovingly call me out when I am not living up to the standards I have set for myself.

These traits help me appreciate my friends and how much they help me become the type of person I want to be. Knowing what I want out of my friendships also helps me release relationships with people who do not build me up in those ways. When you have a strong network of friends—especially female friends—you're less likely to rush into a romantic relationship that isn't right for you or to cling to friendships that don't serve you.

A SELF-LOVE STORY

I like to be around people who possess a certain type of wisdom and who just breathe all of their knowledge into me by being around me and sharing their stories. I hope that I can do the same for them. The most important thing is that you're learning from all your friends all the time.

— Arielle Loren, sexuality writer, documentary
filmmaker, founder of *CORSET* magazine

This Better Be Fun or At Least Have An Open Bar: Show Up Even When You Don't Feel Like It

One of the most popular dating books in the world is *The Rules* by Ellen Fein and Sherrie Schneider. In it, one of the chapters is titled "Show Up Even If You Don't Feel Like It." It's about the importance of getting out and having fun (or at least making a hearty attempt at having fun) if indeed you want to expand your social circle and meet men.

KANEISHA CONFESSIONAL

One night while in grad school, I had the opportunity to experience this important lesson. In a move that was quite out of character of me at the time, I suggested that my girlfriends and I go to a wine tasting and then to salsa lessons at a local club. The reason I say that this was an unusual thing for me to do is that I don't often dance in public by my own volition. I'll go to dance clubs to be social and I'll dance at weddings to prove that I'm a normal, well-adjusted human being. But in general, I do not dance for fun in public. While I've been blessed with a pretty face and a charming personality (if I do say so myself), I was not blessed with as much rhythm as I would've liked. However, I wanted to try something different, and I figured the worst that could happen is that I would clumsily stomp on a few salseros' toes until I could no longer stand to wear my heels, at which point I'd call it a night.

The wine tasting I shuttled us all to turned out to be a tiny event in the cramped back room of a liquor store in a suburb outside of Boston. Still, we got to mingle with fellow twenty-somethings and—

most importantly to us debt-laden graduate students—enjoy free wine.

Afterward, we went out for Thai food, where we had a series of loud conversations about deliciously scandalous topics. It was such a delightful way to spend the evening! As we paid our bill, I began to feel the hermit itch that tells me I want to go home, relax, and watch a movie. You've already missed the 9:00 p.m. salsa lessons, Hermit Kaneisha whispered. You won't be able to catch up by now anyway. Just go another night.

However, one of my friends was determined to go to the salsa club no matter what the rest of us were doing. In fact, one of her friends was having her birthday party at that very same club that night, and she had put all our names on the guest list, freeing us from paying the cover charge. So despite my internal hermit grumblings, we went to the salsa club.

When my friends and I ascended two flights of rickety stairs, I was intrigued to see a wide open room full of standing couples, frozen in anticipation of the dance teacher's next instructions. I immediately knew that I wanted to be there. I imagined my hand matched to a partner's and eyes fixed on the instructor, eager to learn the next move.

To my surprise, an impressively tall and friendly-faced man approached us, introduced himself as a friend of the birthday girl, and whisked me onto the dance floor where he proceeded to teach me the basics of salsa. I have tried to learn salsa before (I lived in Cuba for five months, for goodness sakes!), but this time I actually got it. After three dances with the Salsa Master (I actually called him that to his face), I was in love with salsa.

The rest of the night was pure bliss. Friendly men approached me and my friends and politely asked us to dance. Whenever I got *confused about the steps (which was often), my partners were patient, gracious, and always very encouraging. I knew that in the future, I could show up to this place alone and still have a fantastic time.*

I left the club a hot, sweaty mess with my feet on fire and my heart full of joy. I couldn't wait to go again. I had found a form of dancing that I loved and could actually do (kind of)!

I learned a valuable lesson that night: show up even when you don't feel like it. Maybe it's a dinner you've been invited to. Maybe it's a party or a concert in the park. If you feel yourself exhibiting hermit-like behavior, question where the hermit feelings are coming from. Perhaps you really do need some time alone or with a close friend to rejuvenate. However, if you're feeling any inkling of fear or "smallness," you're most likely letting that little hermit voice talk you out of going. Maybe you're afraid you won't be good at something, afraid you won't fit in, afraid that you won't meet someone, or perhaps, even afraid that you will.

BYOB BROSPECTIVE

The most important way to get into a really fun, heightened state is by getting what I call "socially warmed up." Any time you walk into a party or a bar, try talking to the first person you see. Say, "Hey, how's it going?" Or give a high five. I love high fives. Once you get into that social mode, then it is infinitely easier to get out there and start talking to other people.

— Adam LoDolce, The Dating Confidence Coach
and creator of the film *Go Talk to Her*

Sometimes it isn't our own hermit voice keeping our social lives a dud, but our own friends clipping our social butterfly wings. If you find that your current social circle is hindering the social life you want, here's when you need to speak up. I'll show you exactly what to say with confidence and class.

This Party Sucks, but I Want to Say So Nicely: Scripts to Help You Speak Up for Your Social Life

1. When your friends invite you to the same old not-so-happy hour and you have zero interest in going:

Thanks for thinking of me ladies. I'd love to hang out, but I'm getting tired of the bar scene. Nothing ever seems to change, and we are too fabulous to stay hunched over some sticky bar. I'd love to go out and try something new together if you're interested. If not, I completely understand, but please let me know if you have any other ideas, and we can plan together.

2. When you want to go out on the town to try something new and your friend wants to stay in and watch a movie:

I totally understand if you're interested in more of a chill night in. Tonight I'm feeling energized and excited to go out and mingle, so I'm going to go out even if I have to go alone. Of course you are invited to join me if you change your mind!

SELF-LOVE STORIES

One of my best friends—an excellent BYOBer who inspires me to stay on top of my BYOB game—regularly makes social plans with himself. If no one can join him for something he wants to do, he happily goes out alone.

I love going to the movies by myself. It's very freeing. When you go with a friend or a boyfriend to the movies, someone is always losing out because one person is usually more excited about the movie than the other person. When I go alone, I don't have to worry about that.

— 28 years old, Austin, TX, in a relationship

For him, this regular self-love ritual gets rid of the anxiety of searching for company and the resulting disappointment if he doesn't find it.

Most things I would enjoy doing with other people, but I'm not going to deny myself a wonderful experience just because I don't have someone to experience it with. Always have plans with yourself. It can always be date night with yourself.

My other friend, a thirty-four year-old journalist also from Austin, takes herself out on dates every week.

As much as I would love to be courted, go out on a date, and have a guy drive me somewhere, that's not always possible. The point of my date with myself every week is twofold: one is to celebrate myself for the work that I do. The other part of it is just getting myself into the habit of attracting that positive energy into my life by getting dressed up, going out, and trying something new. That way, when someone does come into my life that I want to date, I'm not out of practice. I know exactly what I'm looking for.

3. When you are out having fun and your friend wants to leave:

I'm having such a great time, and I'm really not ready to leave. I don't want to make you feel like you have to stay, so go ahead and leave without me. Have a good night!

4. When you are out with friends and not having fun, but you still want to go somewhere else before the night is over:

I'm not feeling up to this. I'm going to go look into doing something that's more my speed for tonight. Feel free to join me!

You can leave a place where you aren't having fun even if you don't have a Plan B. Part of being your own boyfriend is letting go of something that doesn't work for you and being fearless enough to improvise. You welcome the uncertainty and realize that it creates space for something unexpected to come along.

The first steps to a better social life are opening yourself up to new activities, finding what you like to do, and showing up even when you don't feel like it. Your inner hermit will eventually give up on pleading with you to stay home. Once you're out and about, do your best to have a good time, remember to speak up when you're dissatisfied, adjust your attitude or gracefully exit if you aren't having fun.

SELF-LOVE PRINCIPLE #24
Figure out what fun means to you and make sure to have lots of it by yourself and with people whose company you enjoy.

Chapter 8:
Protect Your Sexy Self

Be friendly to everybody; protect yourself;
people sometimes want a piece of you
for no good reason; and always
do things out of love not fear.
— RASHIDA JONES

WHILE I AM DELIGHTED that you have begun to unleash your sexy, I also want to emphasize how important it is to protect yourself and be safe. My dad grew up with one younger brother and four younger sisters, so he has a strong protector vibe. He often lectured me on the importance of being able to protect myself in a variety of situations. Several of his sisters have been bitterly disappointed and betrayed by their male partners, and my dad never wanted me to think that just because I was dating a guy that he couldn't one day pose a physical or financial threat to me. Tragically, my youngest aunt was even murdered by her male partner when she was in her early twenties. Thus, my dad drilled into me the importance of knowing how to take care of and protect myself.

My dad never discouraged me from dating, and he has always been nice to guys I've brought home to meet the family. However, he urged me to learn two crucial skills: how to manage my own finances and how to physically defend myself against an attacker. He's a retired corrections officer, and when I was a teenager, he would often test my preparedness with surprise attacks around our house, challenging me to get out of his grip. I usually just laughed it off and rolled my eyes when he tried to show me the various ways to fight off a bigger, stronger attacker. Now that I can count among my friends multiple women who have been mobbed, carjacked, and sexually assaulted by men (sometimes their own boyfriends), I wish I had paid more attention to my dad's impromptu self-defense lessons. What I once thought of as a slightly annoying lecture was actually a critical lesson I am still learning:

SELF-LOVE PRINCIPLE #25

A woman should always know how to protect, take care of, and stand up for herself.

Channel Your Inner Rosie the Riveter: Ways You Should Know How to Protect, Stand Up for, and Take Care of Yourself

There's a big difference between being legally an adult and actually conducting your life as an independent, self-sustaining adult. One of the most important parts of stepping fully into your womanhood is doing your best to take care of yourself. Self-sufficiency is oh-so-sexy.

KANEISHA CONFESSIONAL

I didn't realize how much I depended on men for the smallest tasks until I moved into a house with a thirty-something librarian named Amanda. I had moved into Amanda's house in Baltimore only weeks before James and I broke up. Living with a confident, single woman who owned her own house was exactly what I needed as I began to put back together the pieces of my identity after feeling enmeshed with another person for so long.

To both our horror one day, Amanda and I discovered that a mouse had chewed through a bag of bread in the kitchen. Even though Amanda was deathly afraid of mice (much more than I was), she didn't depend on a man to come over and fix our problem. After much squirming at the thought of the mouse scampering over our counters, Amanda calmly suggested we set mouse traps. Though she had men in her life who could have done our dirty work, she set the example for me of taking care of the rodent ourselves. Similarly, when the electricity in our old brick row home started to act crazy, she called an electrician and immediately had it fixed. Even though these are simple problems that any adult should know how to handle, I realized then that I would have immediately called my current boyfriend or my dad to help me (even though my dad was thousands of miles away!). For once, I was without quick access to a man to rescue me from life's icky errands—and it actually felt great to handle them on my own with my roommate.

Several months later, when I moved in to an apartment by myself in Austin, I realized just how much I had grown from living with Amanda. One morning, the padlock on my front door malfunctioned, effectively locking me in my apartment. I called out to a few passersby from my bedroom window who tried to help, but nothing worked. So I calmly called the fire department. They promptly came over and freed me from my own apartment. It wasn't that I was doing everything by myself now. The big change was that my first thought was no longer to immediately turn to a man in my life to rescue me.

Obviously, it's impossible to be an expert at everything, but it is important that you know how to handle unexpected situations. Here's a list of random things every woman should be prepared to do herself or get taken care of without relying on a boyfriend or a relative. Think of it as a starter to-do list for being a fully confident and independent woman:

- unclog a toilet
- assemble furniture
- set up electronic equipment

- set mouse traps and dispose of them (It's totally okay to do the "This is so nasty!" dance in the process, though.)

- cook healthy (even if very simple) meals for yourself

- speak up for yourself when you are being given poor customer service

- assertively confront anyone who has wronged you, regardless of whether that person is a friend, colleague, or an authority figure (The point here is to be confident enough to do so—not that you have to confront every single person you think has ever offended you.)

- get and keep a job or generate income legally and consistently

- save and budget your money

- understand, file, and pay your taxes

- plan and financially prepare for retirement

- properly use a condom and at least one other contraceptive measure

- drive a car (automatic and manual)

- live for up to two weeks without running water or electricity (I've lived for extended periods of time without running water or electricity, and it is not a game!)

- conduct CPR and basic first aid

- give yourself a monthly breast exam

- change a tire

- jumpstart a car

- get yourself home or to a safe place from wherever you are

- properly use pepper spray (you don't want to end up pepper spraying yourself!)

- defend yourself against a physical attacker

- know where the nearest embassy for your country is when traveling abroad

- introduce yourself and ask for help in the local language of a country you are traveling in

- use a compass and read a map (Google Maps doesn't count!)

- report a crime that has been perpetrated against you

A SELF-LOVE STORY

People think that once you get married or once you're in a relationship, "I don't have to be comfortable being alone ever again because now I have this wonderful person, and we're going to be together forever happily ever after." That is true to an extent, but it's also true that throughout the course of your relationship, you will have times where you have to be more of an independent person, carrying your own weight in the relationship.

— 29 years old, Atlanta, GA, married

Taken 3—Starring You!:
Ways Women Unwittingly Put Themselves in Danger

I'm a very trusting person who loves to socially and emotionally connect with people. This makes me a prime target to be taken advantage of by all kinds of unsavory characters with bad intentions. I learned—sometimes the hard way—that trust must be earned and that even good people can do terrible things. My life experience and community of worldwide readers have taught me that women unwittingly put themselves in danger every day. Hopefully, my common sense reminders to avoid certain dangerous habits will keep you alert and unscathed.

Dangerous Habit #1:
Drinking to excess among relative strangers

One of my favorite dating experts is Patti Stanger, founder of Millionaire's Club, a matchmaking business for wealthy singles. Patti is also the star of a reality TV show on Bravo called *The Millionaire Matchmaker*. On the show, Patti gives her matchmaking clients a two-drink maximum rule on the first date to ensure they don't get sloppy drunk and make fools of themselves. Another reason she discourages overdrinking is to prevent her clients from having casual sex, which she believes hinders the cultivation of true intimacy over time.

I completely agree with Patti's two-drink maximum rule, but I would extend it beyond the first date to the entire duration of the casual dating stage. If you aren't in a committed, exclusive relationship with a man that you know and trust, you should keep your wits about you at all times. In fact, I'd recommend forgoing alcohol altogether in the earliest stages of dating if you can help it. I once read somewhere that the most popular date rape drug is alcohol. From my own experience and that of too many of my friends, that is 100 percent true.

Dangerous Habit #2:
Riding in the same car with a guy you don't know well

When you start dating someone from your college, church, or workplace, you've typically had time to observe him for months before you spend time alone or ride alone in a car with him. However, if you've met someone online, at a club, or any place that hasn't allowed you to observe a man's reactions and behaviors over a period of time, you need to have your own mode of transportation to and from a date. Meet in places like downtown areas where there are plenty of venues to visit within walking distance. Please remember that a whole lotta crazy can hide behind a handsome face!

Dangerous Habit #3:
Sharing cabs with handsome strangers

The popular action thriller *Taken* starring Liam Neeson showed how dangerous it can be to let a stranger know where you live. In the movie, two high school seniors jaunt off to Paris, ready for an adventure. Shortly after arriving at the airport, they run into a handsome, seemingly fun-loving young man who offers to share a cab and invites them to a party. The girls readily agree, giddy over their pending adventure. After noting where the girls live when the cab drops them off, the handsome stranger returns several hours later with several accomplices to kidnap the girls and enslave them as drugged-up sex workers. Though this is a dramatic, fictional example, it's entirely possible and happens every day to real people. Don't let strangers know where you live, ladies, and especially not when you are abroad.

Dangerous Habit #4:
Falling in love while on vacation

I'm not implying that all men you meet on vacation are scam artists, crooks, or married, but enough of them are to warrant seriously thinking twice about a man that sweeps you off your feet while you're on vacation. Your ten-day vacation could easily be a married man's long business trip. Several of my good friends have married wonderful men that they met while studying, working, or vacationing abroad, but I also have other friends who were sexually assaulted, deceived, manipulated, and cheated out of their money by the men they dated while vacationing and living abroad. Crooks anywhere will prey on people who have money to travel and who have let their guard down. Have fun while on vacation, but make sure you are keeping yourself safe while you get your groove back.

KANEISHA CONFESSIONAL

I had my first head over heels, crazy in love experience—or at least what I thought was love—during college while I was studying abroad in Havana, Cuba. When I met "Diego," I was smitten. He was a lovely, coffee-colored, curly-haired, smooth-talking hip-hop artist (or at least that's what he said he was) that I met outside of a movie theater. I gave him the phone number to the house I shared with other students (a foreshadowing of more bad decisions to come), and the next day we met up for a fun date.

From that first date, I was infatuated with Diego. He quickly became my hot Cuban boyfriend. We spent most of our time walking around the city, going out to eat (on my dime) and making out in city parks. I questioned him a few times about why we never went to his house, but he always said that he had lots of roommates and we'd have no privacy (an excuse I readily accepted).

One afternoon, Diego invited me to his place for an afternoon delight, and I excitedly rushed over. I was surprised that none of his roommates were home. When I asked him why he had nail polish and girly linens at his place, he explained that they belonged to his female roommate. Once again, I blindly accepted his explanation, though it actually made no sense ("Oh yeah, I sleep on my roommates' sheets too!"). I brushed all inadequate explanations aside. I felt like I had met my soulmate, my future husband. I even had one of my friends in the States investigate what it would take for Diego and I to get married. (Crazy much?)

My blinders of naïveté were soon shattered when I came home from school one day and a housekeeper gave me an urgent message from Diego's "sister." Diego had never mentioned having a sister, but I called the woman back and spoke with her. She already knew where I lived, which made the entire situation even more strange.

She wanted to come and talk in person, so I waited for her in front of my house.

"As you can tell, I am not Diego's sister," the beautiful woman said dramatically as she approached me in front of my house.

"Um . . . then who are you?" I asked, truly clueless.

"I'm his wife. Here's our marriage certificate and a bunch of your things that you left in my house," the woman said, pulling a stray sock, my mp3 player, and a pack of tampons out of her purse.

I went blind and breathless at the same time. As soon as the words "I'm his wife" came out of her mouth, it all came together for me—his reluctance to having me come to his home, the girly things in his place, his habit of disappearing without notice for days at a time. I felt like such a fool. In an instant, I went from being an exuberant young woman "in love" to a devastated, brokenhearted mess.

"Don't worry," Diego's wife said with sadness and anger brimming in her voice. "I don't want him. You can have him. He is nothing but a lie on two legs."

The months that followed my discovery of Diego's deception were some of the saddest of my life. Like many "women on the side," I had trouble letting the relationship go despite the betrayal I had endured. I held on to Diego even after realizing that the object of my affection was legally bound to someone else. When I left Cuba to return to college, I vowed to never speak to him again, and I didn't. I'm sure he still thinks of me from time to time—that bright-eyed, boisterous American girl that had fallen so hopelessly in lust with him. I only hope that my story saves someone else from the heartbreak I endured.

My story is sad, but it's not original. Women get drawn into relationships with married men all the time. Being "the other woman" is not confined to people traveling abroad, but it's a lot easier for a cheating womanizer to snare you in a web of lies when you are out of your usual element. Make sure that this doesn't happen to you. Have fun on vacation, but don't abandon your common sense.

Dangerous Habit #5:
Having sex without knowing enough about your partner

Another place where many women completely give up all common sense is the bedroom. Even an intelligent, accomplished woman can be a dummy when it comes to protecting her sexual health. How many times have you had sex (a few pumps count!) without insisting that the guy wear a condom? How comfortable are you with inquiring about your partner's sexual history—and how often do you actually do it? And how many times have you regretted letting guys get free samples—you know, when they say, "Just the tip, I promise!" It's a sad fact: women often put their health at risk in the heat of the moment. My love, this is your precious body and it's up to you to protect it.

So how can you protect yourself—really?

1. Wait to have sex.
No, this is not the abstinence until marriage suggestion. I'm advocating that you consider waiting a bit (probably longer than you feel like waiting) before you have sex with someone you are dating. Rather than relying on the "five-date rule," "one-month

rule" or whatever it is, try and prolong the sexy stuff until you really feel like you know and trust the other person. Remember the advice from *The Millionaire Matchmaker*, Patti Stanger: no sex before monogamy!

Ladies, men will wait if they really like you. I have surveyed several of my attractive, straight male friends who all say that they are willing to wait *months*—not just a few dates or a few weeks—to have sex with a woman they really care about. The women I know who have waited around three months to have sex with their partners have wonderful things to say about how strong their relationships turned out. I'm not putting down women who have sex early on in a relationship; I'm merely pointing out that sex early on can cloud your perception of a man's character. We've all gotten light in the head and downright dickmatized by guys who were more like pricks in disguise than the princes of our dreams.

2. Discuss your sexual histories and habits.
No matter what, do not tell your guy "your number" or try to guess at his. Discussing the gory details of how many people you have each been with will only cause drama and awkwardness, and at least one of you will be lying anyway. Instead, talk about what kinds of contraceptive measures you're accustomed to and make sure that both of you agree on using sexual protection. Women should be particularly wary of men who consistently put them in the position of having to be the protection police. If a guy is willing to have sex with you without a condom, he's probably done the same thing with lots of other women.

3. Discuss your sexual health and status early on.
If you make it clear from the beginning that your sexual health is very important to you, the guy has plenty of time to get tested and show you the results before any hanky-panky goes down. He has no excuses not to get tested if you give him plenty of time. Make it clear that this is a prerequisite to getting access to your Little Miss Pretty.

That Doesn't Look So Good . . . : How to Ask Your Boyfriend to Get Tested

Bring up the subject during a quiet evening while you are chilling out and feeling comfortable with one another—and fully clothed. (I'll explain why soon.) Here's a script you can use to ask your partner to get tested:

I think you're really sexy and that I'll be ready to have sex with you soon. My sexual health is really important to me, and I'm sure yours is important to you, too. Before we get intimate, I want you to get tested and show me the results. I will do the same for you. Will you do that for me?

The script may seem overly formal, but it is actually a concise, nonthreatening, and nonaccusatory way to get your point across to your significant other. The specific, pointed question at the end of the script is important because it makes the other person agree to take a specific action rather than simply reply, "Yes, I agree that you should protect your sexual health. Now get buck naked and on your hands and knees!" The important part of the conversation is actually getting the person to agree to get tested and then to *show* you the results *before* you get intimate. A verbal report of his test results won't cut it. You need to see the original documentation from the lab. Though lots of sexually transmitted infections make themselves known with itching and oozing, others go undetected unless you get an actual test.

BYOB BROSPECTIVE

There are so many manipulative things that guys are going to try to pull. Women have to be willing to stand up for what they need and what they want. And they should feel comfortable. If they don't, then either they need to be working on themselves to have the confidence and the self-esteem or they need to be ditching those guys that are pressuring them.

— 28 years old, Los Angeles, CA, dating

Believe Me, He's Not Allergic: Three Ways to Get Your Guy to Wear a Condom

Even if you are on birth control, I recommend also using a condom to protect yourself from most sexually transmitted infections. When I was in graduate school, a nurse recommended that I wait until I had been in an exclusive relationship for at least six months before even considering having sex with a guy without a condom. Whatever timeline you choose (or whether you ever choose) to raw dog it, I want you to always feel empowered to tell a guy to use a condom. After all, if you are willing to let a man put his fingers, tongue, and penis inside of you (graphic much?), you should feel

100 percent comfortable asking him to do something as easy as wearing a condom. He might offer up creative workarounds ("Girl, I got this. They don't call me the pullout king for nothing!") and silly excuses. ("I feel so close to you emotionally, I want nothing to be between us.") If he does, it's completely your prerogative—no, your *responsibility*—to insist that he use a condom or shut down the party. Refuse to continue any sexual play until his sausage is safely wrapped.

A SELF-LOVE STORY

"Jessica," now 30 years old, learned the condom lesson the hard way. She contracted chlamydia in her sophomore year of college from a guy she had thought was The One.

I had this very high school sort of fantasy about things as opposed to living in reality. That STD really brought me back to reality. It really forced me to think, "What are you doing, and who are you doing it for? Is this something that's healthy? Is this something that's loving?" I was like, "No. Enough is enough." I began to change my association with sex and relationships and how they go together.

— 30 years old, Bronx, NY, single

BYOB BROSPECTIVE

Guys have a responsibility to do the right thing. Women have the responsibility to check them on it and make sure they do.

— 28 years old, Los Angeles, CA, dating

Here are three simple and effective ways to get your boyfriend to pause during playtime and put on a condom:

1. Be sexy.

Seductively purr, "It's time to put on a condom. Here, let me put it on for you," and slide it on sensually. Sometimes getting a man to cheerfully wear a condom is like tricking a reluctant kid into taking a bath by adding toys to the tub and making it fun!

2. Be funny.

Depending on the mood of the moment, you can lightheartedly say something like, "So should we name our baby after you regardless of whether it's a boy or a girl?" Then flash him your sweetest smile and slip the condom into his hand. (My personal favorite condom comedy routine is to combine my name with the guy's name and say something like, "Our baby Aaroneisha is going to be adorable. What should her middle name be?")

3. Be direct.

Other times, there is no need to be coy or funny. It should be enough to simply say, "Please put on a condom before we go any further. Thanks!"

Never in my life have I had a man refuse to put on a condom after I made the request. On the other hand, even the nicest guys I have dated have tried to see if I would keep quiet and let him just slip it in. No sir! I'll stay healthy and baby-free for now, thank you very much.

SELF-LOVE PRINCIPLE #26

**Protecting your physical and sexual health
is a powerful and necessary act of self-love.**

Part 3:
Change Your Life

Chapter 9:
Change Starts on the Inside

We delight in the beauty of the butterfly,
but rarely admit the changes it has gone through
to achieve that beauty.
— MAYA ANGELOU

EVERYONE WANTS TO KNOW THE SECRET to getting what you want. Let me tell you this: getting anything you want in life starts with knowing yourself and what you really want. For many people, knowing what they want—or admitting to themselves what they want and then honoring those desires—is the most difficult part of all.

Knowing Yourself before The One

One of the most important life decisions we make will be with whom we choose to be in a romantic relationship and life partnership. Of course, since this book is called *Be Your Own Boyfriend*, I want your first focus to be on making sure the life partnership you have with yourself is strong and healthy. But when all is said and done, most of us are very excited about falling in love and meeting The One.

While all relationships have valuable lessons for us, not all people we are mutually attracted to are meant to be our romantic partners. A good relationship is one where each of you lives in integrity with your own values while building up, supporting, and loving each other. A bad relationship is one where you frequently hurt each other and routinely destroy one other's spirit. In a bad relationship, neither of you are living in integrity with your individual values. While not every relationship is going to be easygoing all the time, it definitely makes life easier to have more good relationships than bad ones.

Strangely, many women are accustomed to filtering potential boyfriends with a checklist of the physical and material qualities they want in a man (e.g., height, build, salary, level of education), but they have not concluded with the same precision what kind of emotional, spiritual, and interpersonal qualities they want in a relationship. A great guy in a bad relationship is a world of heartache for a woman in love. In addition to knowing what kind of man you want, be sure to know what kind of *relationship* you want.

Following this paragraph are some of the qualities in a relationship that make me feel loved, accepted, and secure. While some of the points are more important than others, knowing what I want out of a relationship helps me be honest with myself when a relationship is not working.

KANEISHA CONFESSIONAL

Every time I date a new guy, I get clearer on what I want out of a partner.

- *He is emotionally ready and available for a serious, committed relationship.*

- *He enjoys spending time alone with me but can also have fun spending time by himself or together as a couple out on the town.*

- *He supports and encourages my dreams and harebrained ideas rather than discouraging me or giving me "reality checks" when I am having fun brainstorming.*

- *I can trust him to tell me the truth.*

- *He does not put himself in social situations that would compromise our relationship.*

- *He is dedicated to his physical, spiritual, and mental health. He will enthusiastically participate in activities with me that help us have strong minds, bodies, and spiritual lives.*

- *I am physically and emotionally attracted to him and he to me. We have a fun, active, monogamous sex life.*

- *He is able and willing to travel around the country and abroad with me. He knows how to relax while traveling and will call me out when I'm getting too uptight about sticking to our vacation itinerary.*

- *He enjoys eating my cooking and will help me cook and/or wash the dishes afterward.*

- *He will watch movies that we both enjoy and won't give me a hard time when I watch my beloved indie romance movies alone.*

- *He will enthusiastically discuss books, articles, art, and current events with me.*

- *He gets along and has fun with my loud, fun (and sometimes difficult) family.*

Now it's your turn to make your list. Afterwards, reflect upon these areas in the relationship you have with yourself. In other words, how many of the experiences you want to have with a partner do you provide for yourself?

SELF-LOVE PRINCIPLE #27
**Get clear on what matters most to you
in a romantic relationship. Then make sure
you are living in that experience by yourself
before expecting that experience with a partner.**

Getting clear on what you want could drastically change the way you date, the people you date, and how long your relationships last. As I gained clarity on what I wanted out of a relationship and a partner, I noticed that the time I spent with guys before parting ways was getting shorter and shorter. I went from a four-year on-again, off-again emotional torture match of a relationship to a year-long dysfunctional long-distance relationship. After those two relationships ended, I would typically give it a good three months before calling it quits. After my three-month phase passed, it would often be a few weeks before we said goodbye. I started to worry that I was racing through men and that this was surely a sign that I was doing something terribly wrong. My happily married friend and editor of this book, Millie, put a more positive spin to my situation. She had gone through a similar pattern in her single days, but each time she ended a relationship, she felt relieved she hadn't spent more time with the wrong guy. "You're just getting better at spotting what you want and what you don't want," she said. "You're getting pickier, and that's how it's supposed to be!" Hopefully Millie is right and I'm not just a maneater. The more clear I get about what I want, the less I feel the need to cling to a man who is not right for me.

Playing Tug-of-War with Your Soul: What Are You Resisting?

My very good friend Naeesa is an artist. Her calling is writing fiction and teaching yoga. That is what she was put on this Earth to do. I am an artist as well. I believe I was put on this Earth to prolifically create, to counsel and mentor others, and to influence people through language and ideas. I'm a writer, teacher, public speaker, and a coach. I have so much to learn, and I think a big part of my purpose is sharing what I learn with others. Let's pretend for a second that we're in one of those dystopian sci-fi movies and it is now illegal to write or teach. I would still do them surreptitiously because I love writing and teaching. I would risk my life and my safety to do these things because more than just my profession, writing and teaching is Who I Am. In a way, you could say that those two things are my art.

A few years ago, my fellow artist Naeesa tipped me on to a wonderful book titled *The War of Art* by Steven Pressfield. Steven Pressfield wrote the blockbuster fiction books *Gates of Fire* and *The Legend of Bagger Vance,* but he has also written several books aimed at inspiring and encouraging artists of all kinds. In *The War of Art*, Pressfield takes the reader through a journey of discovering all the different ways the artist's inner enemy, named Resistance, keeps us from doing what we were put on this Earth to do.

By artist, he does not mean you have to be a writer or a painter. Instead, he is referring to any person engaged in a sustained endeavor which elevates her to a higher state of being—any person making an effort to be their best selves.

Resistance takes on many forms, but its main goal is to stand in the way of you and your higher self. Resistance's job is to keep us just as we are, rather than allowing us to develop into the artists we are meant to be. Pressfield advocates that we are all artists in one way or another, meant to masterfully paint our lives as we take risks to express ourselves and freely share our talents with the world. Resistance stands in the way of our art, and it's our job to overcome Resistance lest it overcome us.

KANEISHA CONFESSIONAL

Though I wanted to write books since the day I could read, I buried my dream of being a writer for many years. It started in seventh grade when I switched from the middle school in my neighborhood to a magnet school in a different neighborhood. I went from being the best writer I knew at school to being a strong but unremarkable writer among my new peers at a challenging school full of overachievers. Rather than proudly claiming my territory as a writer, I compared myself to my peers, which led me to become dissatisfied. In my mind, I was average in my imagined hierarchy of good writers in the school. Eventually, I got so distracted by not being "the best" that I completely opted out. In the eighth grade, instead of serving as an editor for the school literary magazine like my English teacher encouraged me to do, I became a cheerleader and took up the alto saxophone in band class. While these activities were fun, neither gave me the satisfaction that writing and working on an editorial team had given me in seventh grade.

Many years later when I went to college, I slowly began to reclaim my dreams of becoming a writer. However, my commitment to pursuing writing was eclipsed by my ambitions to attend Harvard for graduate school. I succeeded at getting into Harvard and once I got there, I was again surrounded by amazing writers—many of whom expressed no desire whatsoever to be professional writers. I could have easily become insecure about my writing ambitions among such natural writing talent. This time, however, I did not shrink away from my dreams; instead, I pursued them with gusto. Now, I'm back in the writing game in full force, and nothing can stop me from fulfilling my destiny. My territory as an artist is the blank page, the unearthed idea, and the student seeking guidance— whether the student lives inside as me or takes on the form of a reader, coaching client, or pupil. I'll be a writer and a teacher for as long as I live. I have finally realized that you don't need anyone to crown you as a writer; as long as you consistently write and share your work with the world, you are indeed a writer. The same goes for being a dancer, singer, painter, or any other kind of artist. You decide that you are an artist. And then you get to keep your title by creating and sharing your art with the world.

Finally having a name for that sneaky saboteur with many disguises has helped me move forward in pursuing my dreams. It's easier to overcome Resistance when I can sense it creeping up on me. Now I can say "Oh hell no, not you again! Get outta here because I have work to do!" Hopefully, you too will now recognize Resistance when it tries to steer you away from doing your work.

You know that you are Resisting your artistic destiny if . . .

1. You have a gnawing sense of dissatisfaction in your life that you keep burying and avoiding.

Do you find it hard to sleep sometimes because you have so many ideas floating around in your brain? Perhaps you never write down those ideas and eventually forget about them. Maybe you do write them down, but you never take the first step to act on them. Do you dramatize your life and indulge in excessive amounts of food, alcohol, sex, relationship strife, familial conflict, or shopping sprees? You are likely creating drama in your life because you are Resisting your artistic destiny and seeking a distraction from the work you know you must do.

2. You feel like a different person was dreaming up your life when you were a kid.

Young children are magical because they have not been socialized into having mediocre expectations for their lives. They dream big because they don't know about mortgages, subscribe to society's gender roles, or care about the odds of success. As an adult, you have bills, dependents, a career to establish and uphold, and "realistic" expectations for your life. That idealistic child who wanted to be a ballerina, veterinarian, inventor, or fashion designer is still inside of you, though she may be buried under years of denial and avoidance. Don't let grown-up filters enable you in Resisting the artist inside of you. Your art doesn't necessarily need to be your job or your full-time income. Don't let this perfectionist misconception or all-or-nothing thinking keep you from pursuing your art.

3. You get sick frequently. You never have enough energy. Or you simply have an inexplicable malaise that nothing seems to alleviate.

Just as doing your art feeds and sustains you, Resisting that art can and will drain the life out of you. The mental, spiritual, and physical energy required for you to pursue your artistic destiny is already within you. If left unused, that energy turns in on you, causing all kinds of problems from restlessness and anxiety to depression, addictions, and body aches.

Resistance takes on a different form for each person, shapeshifting as needed to thwart the full expression of each person's particular gift. The first step to beating Resistance is to identify it for what it is rather than the many ways it disguises itself. Go ahead, call it out on its sabotaging scare tactics! From there, you can work through it consistently and make progress toward your goals one inspired action at a time. Don't seek to understand, dismantle, or argue with Resistance. That just makes it stronger as it gives you a clever way to continue procrastinating. Resistance will fade away as you sit down and do your work! So what are you resisting?

SELF-LOVE PRINCIPLE #28
**Discovering and developing your passions
is a necessary act of self-love.**

Self-Awareness Is Sexy

We've all heard that getting to know yourself is good for the mind, body, and soul. It's also one of the secrets to unleashing your sexy. Here are several ways to help you be more self-aware:

1. Journal regularly.

When you get excited about an idea or have a spark of inspiration, resist the urge to research online (I know about this temptation to impulsively "research" because I am the Queen of Nonsense Googling), call someone at random ("Hey, Grandma! I know you're taking a bath, but I've had an epiphany that I *must* share with you!"), or broadcast your thoughts through social media. The same goes for when you have a problem or a nagging doubt. Before reaching outside, reflect upon it with yourself through journaling. Eventually, you will become your own best friend and thought partner.

2. Meditate and/or pray daily.

Sit in a quiet room in a comfortable position, close your eyes, and quiet your mind. Whenever your mind starts to chatter and wander, return your attention to your breathing. Do this every day for ten minutes and experience the calming "everything is going to be okay" effects of taking time to slow down, be quiet, and receive information from your inner voice.

3. Join a support group or go to counseling if you have been struggling with an unresolved issue.

We all have real-life stories that feature monsters, witches, and dragons that may have harmed us psychologically, physically, emotionally, financially, or spiritually. No matter how dramatic or painful your particular story, you will never experience the freedom that comes with taking responsibility for your own life and your own happiness if you are stuck in the past. Get the professional help you need to heal and move on from past traumas. Trying to "fix yourself" by reading self-help books (even one as good as *Be Your Own Boyfriend*) can't substitute help from a licensed practitioner coupled with a structured support group.

4. Get insight into your personality.
Read books that relate your personality type to other facets of your life (i.e., career choice, relationship dynamics, etc.) For years, I saw myself as this wildly different, unknowable, unpredictable person. When I took an adaptation of the Myers Briggs Type Indicator test, I learned that I was an ENFP (extroverted intuitive feeling perceiver). Reading personality test results that described me in detail gave me a tremendous sense of comfort. I wasn't as crazy as I thought! I was just a certain "type" of person, and there were millions of other people in the world just like me. It also gave me a lens through which I could understand other parts of myself, including the kinds of jobs I was best suited for and the kinds of people I was most compatible with for friendship and romance.

5. Ask your friends, family, and mentors to describe your greatest strengths and weaknesses.
Remember to accept their opinions with an open heart and open mind without letting their feedback inflate or deflate your sense of self too much. Pay attention to your immediate reactions and how you feel about the feedback you receive. Sometimes your reaction

to the feedback you get reveals more about you than the feedback itself.

A SELF-LOVE INSIGHT

My mom always says, "Only your family will tell you the truth," and she usually means that only your family will tell you the UGLY truth.

— 26 years old, Washington, DC, in a relationship

6. Remove yourself from your everyday environment.

It's easy to think of yourself in relation to the people and responsibilities you have in your life. "I am so-and-so's daughter, sister, mother, boss, employee, etc." or "I am a graduate of this college, belong to this or that race, class, religion, etc." While all of the aforementioned qualities are parts of your life experience, your roles, responsibilities, degrees, and creed do not define you.

Who you are is what is left when all of society's labels and expectations fall away and you are free to just be. Give yourself the opportunity to see the person you become if you travel forty or 4,000 miles away. See how you feel when you spend a day in an unfamiliar part of town. Even if you have a very demanding job, make the effort to eat an atypical meal for lunch in a different area of the office building. Notice if you relate to people differently than you normally would. This could be a usually hidden part of you taking the opportunity to make herself known.

SELF-LOVE PRINCIPLE #29

**A routine is not the same as an identity.
Break out of your routine to uncover your true identity.**

When you step into your "alternative identity," you may notice that you are more relaxed, calm, creative, open-minded, friendly, or courageous. Mindfully bring whatever desirable elements you experienced during that "time off" of being your usual self into your everyday identity. The way we think, speak, act, dress, spend our time, and interact with our environment are all elements that contribute to our identity. If there is something about your public persona that doesn't make you feel like your best self, feel free to release that belief or behavior and change it.

SELF-LOVE PRINCIPLE #30

**The first step to knowing what you want
is knowing who you are.
Dedicate time to get to know yourself
and get clear on what you want.**

BYOB EXPERT ADVICE

To me, self-awareness is very different from self-judgment. Self-awareness is being aware of the key concept that we're spiritual beings having a human experience. We're aware that everything that's happening to us is for our highest good. And self-awareness is also about self-responsibility—not blaming other people and not expecting other people to fix us. No one can cause our pain and no one can make us happy. These are all things that we do ourselves. To me, that's self-awareness.

— Christine Hassler, inspirational speaker, life coach, author of
The 20 Something Manifesto and *20 Something, 20 Everything*

Chapter 10:
Keep It Simple, Sexy

Simplicity is the keynote of all true elegance.
— COCO CHANEL

SOMETIMES, WE SMART GIRLS can make life much more complex than it needs to be. As I have matured, I have realized how fun it can be to just relax, and approach each challenge as it comes my way rather than trying to predict what might be on the horizon. I'm learning to live my life one day at a time. When your energy isn't tied up in being perfect or trying to control the outcome of everything, you have a lot more energy to pour into loving yourself, loving others, and loving your life.

Are You a Maximizer or Satisficer?

I first learned about the terms maximizer and satisficer from the book *Marry Him: The Case for Settling for Mr. Good Enough* by Lori Gottlieb. In it, she explores what makes certain people comfortable with the "good enough" solution to a problem and what drives other people to relentlessly drive to perfection. Specifically, she explores why some women (herself included) have the habit of always looking for a "better" partner. Barry Schwartz also explores maximizers and satisficers at length in his book *The Paradox of Choice*. When faced with decisions, every person is primarily a satisficer or a maximizer. Satisficers face a particular situation and seek a solution that addresses the situation in a "satisfactory" way. Satisficers aren't lazy. Nor do they necessarily have low standards. They just know that they have limited time, energy, and resources to apply to the hundreds of decisions we all make every day. Satisficers keep this reality in mind, and adjust their expectations accordingly. Once a satisficer finds a "good enough" solution, she moves on with her life without feeling any nagging sense of what could have been.

On the other hand, maximizers face every situation with the attitude that they need to get the absolute best possible solution to the problem. Even when they have found a good enough solution— or sometimes even a great solution—they persist in looking for a better option. According to one of my favorite bloggers, Penelope Trunk, satisficers are happier people, whereas maximizers tend to be more interesting people.

Each personality type has its own benefits. Maximizers can be great at bringing out the best in themselves and others. Maximizers push themselves and others to greater heights of achievement. How good would a basketball coach be if he let his players stop practice once their shooting skills were "good enough"? Conversely, satisficers are great at stopping the mad dash to perfection, thus conserving energy, time, and resources for other pursuits. The trick is to learn when it serves you to be a maximizer and when you'd be better off as a satisficer. We all tend to lean one way or the other naturally, but I like to think that we can mindfully choose to be maximizers or satisficers depending on the situation.

Review the following scenarios and see if you identify more with the thought process of the satisficer or the maximizer.

Scenario #1:
Going to the movies with friends

Satisficer: When choosing a movie to watch with friends, I watch a few trailers, read a few movie reviews, and pick a movie as soon as we all find one we think we'd enjoy seeing. Sometimes, I don't watch trailers or read reviews at all. If someone else has a movie they'd like to see and it sounds interesting, I'll give it a try.

Maximizer: Choosing a movie usually takes me a long time. I need to read a lot of reviews, watch several trailers, and find the movie theater with the most comfortable seats, the tastiest popcorn, as well as the most convenient showtime. I also want to check if there are any discounts that we can use. Once all that is settled, I feel comfortable heading out to the theater. Yes, sometimes the process takes a lot longer than it needs to, but when I check off all those things on my mental list, I know I'm going to have the best possible experience.

Scenario #2:
Choosing a restaurant for your birthday dinner

Satisficer: Since there will be six of us at the dinner, I want a place that will comfortably fit all of us and have food that most people will enjoy and can afford. One of my favorite restaurants already meets all of the criteria, so I'll call and make a reservation there because I know we'll all have a good time. Now I can relax and enjoy the rest of my day off, knowing that everything is taken care of.

Maximizer: Since there will be six of us at my birthday dinner, I want a restaurant that can seat us in a private area where we can laugh, talk, and celebrate as loudly as we please. There should also be enough variety on the menu that everyone can find their favorites, but not too much variety that ordering is going to be overwhelming. Most of my friends have already been to all of my favorite restaurants and I want this to be a special occasion, so I need to find a place that's new for everyone. However, since I've never been to the restaurant myself, I need to read lots of reviews to make sure the food is to die for and the ambiance is mellow candlelit chic. And lastly, since I bought a hot new dress for my birthday, the restaurant should be the type of place where people dress up. Yes, this process is more complicated and time-consuming than just choosing a place I already know and like, but in the end, I can be sure that we'll all have a new experience together and celebrate in style.

Scenario #3:
Buying a plane ticket to visit your parents

Satisficer: I really enjoyed my Virgin America flight the last time I flew, so I'm going to check if they have flights in my budget for the dates I need to fly. If not, I'll look for Southwest Airlines flights because I know that they always have affordable flights. Either way, I hope to get a window seat so I can sleep soundly.

Maximizer: I always get the best flight when I travel. First, I check the fares on multiple price comparison sites. Then I find which flight is the cheapest, shortest duration, and has the most convenient departure times for me. If the flight is going to have a layover, it should be at an airport that I'm familiar with and that has at least one healthy meal option. Once I find a flight that works for me, I then go to the airline website to double-check the airline's direct price. I go with the cheaper one, of course. Once my flight is settled, I choose the best seat. For me, that means a window seat as close to the front of the plane as possible. If I find a window seat next to a vacant one, I would go for that one, hoping nobody buys the seat next to me. Buying a flight can be exhausting, but it's worth it if I get the most bang for my buck.

Scenario #4:

Deciding whether or not to continue a courtship with someone you've been casually dating

Satisficer: I never would have seen myself dating a guy like him, but here I am! He isn't as tall or muscular as the guys that usually attract me, but he's attractive in his own way. Sometimes, things can get a little awkward when it's time for us to choose a dinner spot because he doesn't know much about the food I like to eat. He grew up eating all-American middle-class fare like spaghetti, chicken fried steak, and meatloaf. However, he's usually very open-minded and adventurous when I suggest that we try out a local ethnic restaurant. He makes me feel special. I trust him completely, and the more I get to know him, the more I realize how much he cares about the environment, which is admirable. Since we've only been dating for six weeks, I don't want to jump to any conclusions about him or the potential for our relationship. The more I get to know him, the more positive things I discover about his character. I want to see what happens with us, even if he isn't the type of guy I usually date.

Maximizer: It's been six weeks, and it's probably time to break it off. He isn't as tall or toned as the guys I usually date. I'm worried that as he gets older, his figure will only get worse because he doesn't go to the gym (although he does love to hike and run). I get embarrassed when we go to restaurants because he always asks the waitress to explain items on the menu like he's a little kid! Yes, he knows a lot about nature and building things that I have no idea about, but sometimes I wonder if we really match. Though it's been fun dating him and he's very romantic, I never envisioned myself with a guy like him. He just seems so . . . average. I should probably let him go so I can find someone as exceptional as I am. He should be with someone more "vanilla" to match him.

In all three of these examples, the satisficer has a certain openness about life and its possibilities that the maximizer refuses to entertain out of fear that she will choose a lesser option. Even though the maximizer may win in the short term with her complex decision-making strategies, my prediction is that she will end up significantly less happy than the satisficer in the long term. The maximizer spends too much time making every decision. People become tired of her endless quest for perfection and begin to bow out of close relationships with her. She may stop getting invited to the movies, have a difficult time finding travel buddies, and be puzzled about why a catch as amazing as she is still single. The maximizer doesn't understand that every experience and decision in life doesn't have to be maximized. Sometimes good enough is enough—or even better than endlessly striving for perfection.

The satisficer often has the delightful experience of being surprised at how great something turns out because she approaches each challenge with the expectation that things will work out— even if not perfectly.

I am naturally a maximizer, and I agree that my life has been more interesting than happy. It's not that I'm a notably unhappy person; it's just that I naturally choose the option that will lead to an interesting outcome or a good story. However, I cringe when I think about how overly complicated I can make a simple task.

If your goal is to be happy, it would serve you to try and take on satisficer tendencies in many parts of your life where maximizing is just not that important. It's like that book *Don't Sweat the Small Stuff*. Don't maximize the small stuff.

How to Know When You've Gotten to Good Enough

An important part of curbing excessive maximizer tendencies is to recognize when you are in maximizer mode and consider whether this is the appropriate approach for the situation. The next time you are making a decision—whether you're out shopping for clothes or job hunting online—ask yourself the following questions:

- What is the additional benefit of getting to perfection over what I have now? How much do those additional benefits *really* matter to me?

- What might I lose in the process of striving toward perfection (e.g., time, energy, attention)?

- Am I willing to lose out on other things for the chance to get the perfect outcome?

Sometimes, the difference between a good enough solution and a perfect solution is imperceptible. Are you really going to have a significant difference in your quality of life by driving an extra mile to get the gas that is five cents cheaper? Is losing that last five pounds going to make you *that* much happier? In working toward perfection, you are likely losing time and money that you could use to do something that may actually matter more to you.

More questions to ask yourself as you consider whether you want to stop at good enough are:

- What do I stand to gain by stopping here at the "good enough" solution rather than seeking perfection?

- How does finding the perfect solution compare to what I stand to gain by stopping here at the "good enough" solution?

For example, perhaps you haven't found the absolutely perfect apartment that you want to live in for the next three years, but you have found one that is in your price range, has the amenities you need, and is in the neighborhood that you want to live in. If you stop your search now, you can save your time and energy and stop sleeping in your childhood bedroom. Even better, you can finally get your precious things out of storage. Rather than running around looking for the perfect apartment and risk losing the one you've already found, you can begin to make the good enough one your new home. More questions to consider are:

- What are the worst things that could happen if I accept this "good enough" solution?

- Can I live with these consequences and still be happy?

It's important to think through the real consequences of choosing the good enough solution rather than the imagined consequences of misery and failure that most maximizers attach to anything less than perfect. Once you take the time to think about the worst scenario that could happen if you stop at good enough, you realize that your good enough decision may not be so bad after all. The one question that usually helps me get clear on whether I should continue searching or settle down is:

- How relieved would I be if I stopped searching and settled for the good enough solution that I already have?

Trying to have the best of everything is exhausting and stressful. How much happier might you be if you gave yourself a break and experienced the relief that comes with making a decision and being happy with it? Sometimes, the best things in life are the things we already have and are not fully appreciating. Rather than looking for the best of everything, focus on making the best out of what you already have.

Leave Drama Where It Belongs

In the book-turned-romantic comedy *He's Just Not That Into You*, the main character, Gigi, does everything at the last minute. One of the other characters calls her on it by saying something like: "You love drama. You wait until the last minute to do everything to feel the adrenaline rush to see whether you will make the deadline or not."

This description fit me perfectly when I was in college and then graduate school. Every paper, problem set, and project was finished at the last minute—or after an extension. Similarly, my mom has been hounding me about my love for last-minute races to the finish line ever since I was in middle school, whether it was staying up all night to do a science project or frantically rushing to catch a flight. When I saw that movie, I recognized myself in Gigi in many ways. I finally had to admit: I. LOVE. DRAMA.

In the past, I was often called a drama queen by the men I dated, and I resisted the title. I didn't want to be thought of as high maintenance. However, the subset of my girlfriends who have tumultuous love lives similar to mine have all admitted that deep down, we all love drama. It's not that we want to be miserable and agonized; we just find drama exhilarating and thrilling. We all know that giving in to drama is not the path to happiness. However, I now know that there is a place for drama; it's just not in my daily life—especially not my love life. One guy I briefly dated once said something to me that had a profound impact on me, and I want to pass it on to you.

SELF-LOVE PRINCIPLE #31
A lot of things are going to happen in your life. There will be plenty of drama and unexpected challenges to deal with. Don't look for or create drama where drama isn't necessary.

If you're wondering whether you might be a drama queen, consider the following:

- Do you often wait until the last minute to do important tasks like filing taxes, submitting job applications, and refilling your birth control prescription?

- In your dating life, do you find yourself having a lot of heartfelt talks about "the relationship" rather than taking it slow and simply experiencing the relationship?

- Do you find that you tell the same story more than twice in a week, sometimes even to the same person by accident?

- When bad things happen to you, do you immediately call a friend and tell her about it before reflecting upon it and processing it by yourself?

- When watching dramatic, heart-wrenching movies like *Closer*, do you think, *Oh wow, that's my life*?

- Have you been repeatedly told that you like drama or exaggerate your problems?

If you answered yes to three or more of those questions, you are definitely in love with drama. This is not an entirely bad thing. It just means that you have to channel that drama-loving energy to the right places. Use drama as an asset to your life rather than a liability and a troublemaker!

To make your love for drama work for you rather than against you, try the following:

Creative writing. Instead of creating or magnifying drama in your real life, write fiction. The possibilities are endless. Use your inspiration for short stories, novels, poems, plays, or screenplays. You could submit your stories to contests and even win money! I wrote a very dramatic short story while in college and won $800 for it. My creative writing teacher at the time was David Foster Wallace, the famous American novelist best known for his 1996 book *Infinite Jest*. He called my story "so seductive, you don't even care about the mistakes." Now, that's the kind of drama that pays off.

Acting. There are plenty of small theater companies that would love to have you try out for a part. Release some of that dramatic energy on the stage. If memorizing lines isn't your thing, join an improv troupe. You'll most likely come out of the experience with a newfound fearlessness, new friends, and a healthy outlet for your dramatic flair.

Mentoring or tutoring at-risk youth. You will be amazed and dismayed at the amount of unwanted real-life drama many young people encounter every day. Helping them succeed in school despite their drama will show you what real drama is and give you an appreciation for your relatively drama-free life. It will also get you thinking more about being of service to others rather than focusing on yourself and your own problems. While at Harvard, I volunteered as a weekend program instructor with the nonprofit Citizen Schools. It was a rewarding experience and pulled my energy away from creating drama and toward thinking of creative ways to inspire and educate the students.

Journaling. As you can tell, I'm a big fan of journaling. If you take the time to write about your thoughts and feelings and hash out every dramatic detail of what happened to you in a day, you may find yourself getting tired of focusing on your own drama. Drama Queen-type drama is never really that interesting for long because it is rooted in fear rather than love, abundance, and substance. Once you have journaled about it in extensive detail, you may find yourself less interested in rehashing the story repeatedly to your friends.

Therapy. Counselors are paid to listen to people's drama and then help them work through it and move on. Most insurance plans subsidize at least a few sessions of mental health care. Furthermore, if you are a student, you can likely get a number of sessions for free through your school's on-campus mental health center. A counselor might be exactly what you need to release those dramatic tendencies, and put your attention to better use in your life.

These are just a few tips for giving your inclination toward drama a healthy outlet. Get that image out of your head that you're on a movie screen! Always be conscious that you're dealing with real people with real feelings and there are always consequences. After all, no matter how dramatic a movie is, the pain ends after two hours. When you attract drama into your real life, the damage you inflict on yourself and others can last for years.

Slow Down

I don't know when it happened, but at some point, someone hit the fast-forward button on our lives. We answer emails within a minute of receiving them. We order a book online and want it the next day. We meet someone at an online dating site and want to meet up with them that same evening. It's like we've all decided that faster, faster, faster is better. But think of how many things are so much better when done slowly. Eating slowly helps you know when you are full so that you don't overeat. Slow sex (at least for me!) is often much more enjoyable than slamming into one other frantically. Slow travel allows you to experience the feeling of living in a foreign place rather than shuttling yourself from one tourist attraction to another. In many of life's pursuits, I find that the slow way is simply more enjoyable.

One easy thing you can do today that will change your life is to slow down and be more present. Be mindful of your breathing. Pay attention to the way you carry your body. Take pause and survey your thoughts, and make sure they are the kinds of thoughts you want to be thinking. To me, slowness equates to the notion of loving-kindness found in Buddhism and other spiritual traditions. Think of how you or others behave when you're in a rush. You're easily irritated, annoyed at others who get in your way. Everything seems to be going wrong. Everybody seems like they're out to get you. When you slow down, you have the presence of mind to appreciate the people and environment surrounding you and the deliciousness of your own thoughts and ideas. Slowness gives you the space and the patience to move through the world with kindness and love toward others and yourself.

A SELF-LOVE INSIGHT

Until you can have those moments where you can appreciate, savor, and enjoy, it is difficult to find what your passion is and to find love and caring.

— 30 years old, Bronx, NY, single

Why to Say No

Part of slowing down is to not have the knee-jerk reaction to say yes to every request that is made of you. Saying no is one of the most powerful things you can do for yourself. Many women have a hard time saying no because we're naturally inclined to help others before we nurture ourselves. Meet every opportunity with gratitude while being mindful of your own desires, time, and energy. Here are several reasons why you should learn to exercise your "no" muscle.

1. You'll have more time to yourself.
Do you often feel tired, stressed out, and like you're constantly running from one thing to the next? It's because you keep saying yes to everything! Fabulous women need time to cultivate our luscious lives: sleep, do our hair, read a great book, take a bubble bath, clean our apartments, cook ourselves a delicious meal, do yoga, watch a movie, paint while drinking wine, go shopping, and write in our journals. When you say yes to every party invitation, volunteer event, and comply with every requested favor from a friend, you end up losing time to nurture your mind, body, and soul, as well as crucial time you need to run simple errands.

2. You'll teach other people about your boundaries.

People in our lives will encroach on our personal space and time as much as we let them. Those people include work colleagues, managers, clients, friends, boyfriends, and family. It's not that they have bad intentions. If you don't want your time eaten up by a litany of requests and obligations, then you must set your boundaries confidently and consistently. By saying no more often, you'll find that people won't have you at the top of their go-to list for every little favor. It doesn't mean that they'll think you are selfish or rude. They will just know that you protect your time and space and are not immediately responsive to surprise requests.

3. You'll empower those around you.

You can say no and still be helpful by pointing people to another resource. When you stop rushing to do everything for everyone, you create the opportunity for people to find other resources and answers outside of you.

4. You'll say yes to the important things.

When you say no to revamping your friend's resume, you say yes to having two precious uninterrupted hours to work on your novel. When you say no to ironing your man's clothes for the week, you'll likely have more energy to have sex with him that night. (Every married guy I know would take sex with his wife over crisply ironed shirts any day.) When you say no to your colleague's last-minute request to stay late for a meeting, you say yes to taking your dog to the off-leash park.

Ways to Say No

You know I love giving you sample scripts for tricky situations. Those of you who have a difficult time saying no can use these tools to help you confidently stand your ground. Below are a few examples of hypothetical situations and how I'd recommend you deliver your polite but firm no. Short and simple responses work best.

1. Someone invites you to an event you don't want to attend:

Thank you so much for the invitation, but I'm going to pass this time.

2. Someone requests you to do a favor that will suck your time or energy:

I'm not available to do that.

3. Someone asks you to do something that he or she is fully capable of doing:

Thanks for thinking of me, but I know you can handle this without me.

Do not offer an explanation or apology for why you are saying no. It will create the illusion that you are open to negotiating or feel bad about establishing boundaries. Say no pleasantly yet firmly, without accusation or indignation. If it makes you feel better, point them to some helpful resources or to someone else who could be of help. Your friend may be taken by surprise or get a little hurt or angry. This too shall pass.

There is no need to feel guilty about declining a request. Saying no is not the equivalent of any of these:

- I don't like you.

- I don't know how.

- I will never do a favor for you ever again.

You are simply saying no to this particular request. And remember: it's more kind and respectful to give a prompt no than to hem and haw and end up never getting back to someone, which is what often happens to folks who have trouble saying no. Take back your time and energy one no at a time.

Chapter 11:
Life Is Your Magic Genie.
Name Your Wish.

When you want something,
all the universe conspires
in helping you to achieve it.
— PAULO COELHO

I KNOW IT MAY SOUND EXTRA WOO WOO, but I truly believe that you can have anything that you want in life as long as it doesn't encroach on another person's well-being and happiness. It's not about whether or not you can have what you want but whether you actually know what you want and believe that you can have it. So let's first sit down together and get into the nitty-gritty of determining what you want in life.

Mansion-Apartment-Shack-House:
Determining What You Want

Some of us have silenced our inner voice and buried our hopes and dreams under heaps of expectations our family, friends, and society have hoisted upon us. If this has happened to you, it's time to take a deep breath and get in touch with what you really want. Below are some topics I encourage you to think and journal about. By journaling and reflecting upon the issues below, you allow yourself to explore how prospective options feel when you think about them. You get increasingly clear on your life vision. Do not get anxious if you don't have an immediate response to each question. Let it marinate in your mind over several weeks or months as you have more experiences, gather more information, and gain more clarity. Some of these issues may even take you *years* to decide. If an issue causes you discomfort, don't worry. You can revisit the question later. Knowing what matters most to you will help you make decisions that move you closer to your goals.

- Do you want to be legally married, in a domestic partnership, or in some other partnership arrangement?

- Do you want children? If so, why, when, and how many? What are your philosophies on raising and disciplining children?

- What are your spiritual and/or religious beliefs? How important is it to you that your partner share these beliefs?

- Do you want to live in an urban, suburban, or rural environment? Do you want to live in the same place all year or switch homes with the seasons?

- Do you want to live near your parents and other family members or would you rather have some distance?

- Do you want to live in your home country or would you rather live abroad? If you want to live abroad, where do you want to live and for how long?

- How often do you want to travel, and what is your travel style—luxury, shoestring, all-inclusive, slow travel, or some combination?

- What is your ideal vacation and how often do you want to take vacations?

- Do you want to have a high-powered career, be self-employed, run a huge business, work part-time, or be a stay-at-home wife and/or mother?

- What kinds of people do you want to work with on a daily basis in your job?

- What kind of impact do you want the work that you do to have in the world? Do you want to be making a company millions of dollars with your innovative ideas, helping women in developing countries start businesses, teaching children, or creating art? As Howard Thurman once said, "Don't ask what the world needs. Ask what makes you come alive, and do that. Because what the world needs is more people who have come alive." What makes you come alive?

- Do you want to be part of a two-income household, be the breadwinner, or marry someone who is happy to financially support the entire family?

- How important to your happiness is being able to afford certain material possessions (e.g., jewelry, a fancy car, or a big house)?

- How important to your happiness is autonomy over how you spend your time? How do you like to spend your free time?

- What sacrifices are you willing to make to get the things you want in your life? What compromises are you not willing to make?

A SELF-LOVE STORY

One of my interviewees talked about a line from the song *Landslide* by Fleetwood Mac: "I've been afraid of changing because I've built my life around you."

Sometimes I feel like that. I wonder, "How much of my life is the way it is now because I'm in this long-term relationship?" I don't ever want to look back and think that I missed out on something because I was in a relationship trying to meet the needs of the relationship before my own needs.

— 27 years old, New York City, NY, in a relationship

Ways to Research Your Life Options

Some people have a strong sense of exactly what they want out of life. However, if you're like me, you tend to ponder different visions of happiness, adding to the picture as you learn more about yourself. Here are some ways you can research your life options and see how different manifestations of happiness feel to you.

1. Talk to people whom you admire.
Reach out to people who are where you want to be in a certain area of your life and learn how they got there. Whether it's someone who runs a business she loves, someone who is happy and single, or someone who has a close-knit family like the one you want, it can be very helpful to identify role models. Life mentors can help you think through your decisions by sharing their insights and experiences. You don't have to approach someone and ask that person to officially mentor you, though that's fine too. You can simply find ways to surround yourself with people whose lives reflect qualities that appeal to you and ask them questions.

You will find that some people will be more responsive and open than others—and the most responsive people who seem most interested in engaging with you can develop into your informal mentors. Speaking to others about their experiences is not about trying to copy another person's path; it expands your awareness of the options available to you. It's also important to remember that a role model or life mentor does not have to look like you. Some of my most influential role models and life mentors are middle-aged white men! What matters most is that you can turn to that person for candid advice and much-needed encouragement.

2. Consult with a spiritual leader.

Many religious and spiritual traditions prescribe and describe the ideal conditions for family, work, and daily life. Rather than feeling like you have to come up with the answers all alone, seek guidance from a leader in your spiritual community. Even if you don't have a personal relationship with a spiritual leader, you can take on a spiritual mentor who lives far away or lived long ago. Identify someone from the past or present whose ideals appeal to you. Read about how that person describes a good life and how to achieve it. Be open. You don't have to share *all* of a religion's beliefs to learn some valuable gems of wisdom from that particular faith.

3. Envision it.

I am a huge proponent of stimulating your mind and spirit with vivid images depicting what you want. Whether it's a daily affirmation that you read, a vision board, a collage of magazine cutouts, a binder of newspaper clippings, etc., find ways to surround yourself with visual reminders of what you want in your life. These visual cues will subconsciously motivate you to move toward your goals. They will also serve as delightful reminders when you accomplish those goals and see the very things you wished for manifested in your life.

4. Try it out.

Though I think plenty of great advice can and should be taken without having to make the mistake of "living through it" first, experience is often an excellent teacher. Even if you try something and don't like it, you're better off knowing for sure that you do not like something rather than just musing about it. Some decisions are more conducive to experimentation than others. For example, I do not recommend "trying out" having kids, getting married, or even moving in with a man unless you are absolutely ready to accept the serious emotional and financial responsibilities that come along with those kinds of life-changing decisions. However, when it comes to choosing your career or where you want to live, you have more freedom to try them out before committing yourself to one option.

One of the most important things to remember when researching your life options is to allow yourself to believe that you can have anything you want. What helps me buy into this brazen notion is that I know that I can have anything I want—but it's likely that I can't have *everything* that I want all at the same time. Balancing these two things—having anything I want but not necessarily all at the same time—helps me clarify what is most important to me in my life at a particular point and what I'm willing to do without. Most importantly, keep your mind and heart open to possibilities you may not have even considered.

A SELF-LOVE INSIGHT

Clarity is a blessing, but it doesn't come for free generally. You have to find it. Once you find it, everything else comes so much easier.

— 27 years old, New York City, NY, in relationship

Tell Your Story As You Want It to Be

One of my favorite books is Esther and Jerry Hicks's book *Money, and the Law of Attraction.* The law of attraction book series written by this amazing couple was the inspiration for the bestselling book and video *The Secret.* One of the main lessons of Esther and Jerry Hicks's book is that if you want to change circumstances in your life, you must first change your thoughts, which will in turn change your feelings. You have to retell your story as you want it to be rather than as you are experiencing it now. This advice is especially important when applying it to your love life because we often bring our past experiences into our present life by rehashing stories, mulling over what went wrong, and being hypervigilant in new situations so that we won't be hurt and disappointed again.

SELF-LOVE PRINCIPLE #32

If you want different results in your love life, you have to change the story that you are currently telling to yourself and to other people.

It may feel strange and somewhat fake at first, but changing the way you talk about your love life is the only way you are going to align your attitude, spirit, and the abundance of the Universe to bring you what your heart most desires.

I am not asking you to go around telling people outright lies about your love life. (Cuckoo, anyone?) Rather, whenever you have the chance to share your "story" in some way, choose to feel good about your love life and attract to yourself what you want. For example, if you see a romantic restaurant that you'd love to go to with a boyfriend, say to yourself, "I can't wait to go there one day with my partner." And then instead of waiting for a man to invite you there, get dressed up, make a reservation, and go there yourself. While there, consider all the menu items you and your partner would order. You can take it one step further and even order meals for both of you, and take the leftovers home. It may sound a little wacky but visualization combined with an authentic belief in the possibility of receiving what you want are surefire ways to bring what you want to you.

On the other hand, the woman who is determined to be overly realistic and "tell it like it is" ends up with a sad story that sounds like this when she passes that same restaurant: "I wish I could go there, but I don't have anyone to go with. I'm single and all my girlfriends are either too busy with their men, bitter, or broke. All the men I know are too lazy or disinterested to accompany me to a place like that. I guess I'll never go." Retell the story of your love life and genuinely feel good about it even before you've experienced it.

Even if this exercise seems silly, weird, or ludicrous to you, suspend your disbelief and try to have fun with it. Taking the time to sit down and retell your love story is especially helpful if you are feeling dissatisfied and confused in your love life, wondering where all the men are, why other people get their happy endings and yours keeps eluding you.

Note: do not include a long list of must-haves and dealbreakers. Instead, affirm the traits and experiences you hope to have. Focus on what you want. Feel good about it. Believe that you can have it. Make it your new story in your mind and in your actions—and one day, you'll look up and realize it has actually come true.

SELF-LOVE PRINCIPLE #33
**Focus on what you want rather than what you do not want.
Envision getting what you want as vividly as you can.**

Cha-ching! How to Manifest Money

Even as recently as five years ago, my best friends and I would often sit around and muse about how fantastic it would be to marry a fabulously wealthy man who could fund all of our entrepreneurial ambitions and the adventurous lifestyles we craved. Oddly enough, we were graduate students in professional programs at top schools, which were preparing us for fancy six-figure jobs. We didn't picture ourselves becoming independently wealthy. However, a creative life of wealth and freedom was a dream we imagined we would reach through our partners.

It only took one long-term relationship with a fellow Harvard graduate who was unemployed for nearly a year to snap me out of my fantasies of being a kept woman. Watching my then-boyfriend struggle to pay his bills while my own savings dwindled to nothing made me determined to become rich on my own accord. I realized that it was no one else's responsibility to take care of me or fund my dreams. If I wanted to be wealthy and free, the onus was on me. A partner who could share in this with me would be icing on the cake, but it was no longer my plan.

Knowing how to effectively save, manage, and grow your money are all very important parts of being rich and being your own boyfriend. Unfortunately, this is not something that I can teach you because I'm still in the beginning stages of learning how to do it well myself! However, I am proud to say that after two full years of being a struggling writer and entrepreneur, I don't depend on a partner or my parents to fund my dreams or my daily life. With the help of bookkeeping software and my CPA, I keep track of my personal and business expenses and take care of my taxes. I've gone from struggling to pay my rent to being an employer, and that feels great. For sound financial advice I can actually follow, I look to practical, tough love money experts like Suze Orman and Ramit Sethi. Websites like LearnVest, founded by my former Harvard classmate Alexa Von Tobel, provide personal finance and money education for women. These are all great resources for the money skills I am not yet qualified to teach you.

While my budgeting, saving, and investing skills are still a work in progress, my ability to manifest money is quite strong. *This*, my friend, I am excited and highly qualified to teach you. My main income for the last two years has been helping people get into top graduate schools, which means most of my money came in the form of new clients. Whenever I wanted an influx of money, I followed a series of steps that I developed through self-education and my own money manifestation experiences. Old-school texts like *Think and Grow Rich* by Napoleon Hill and *The Science of Getting Rich* by Wallace Wattles taught me the secret to using the Universe like my own personal ATM.

I manifest money by creating an environment of financial abundance and gratitude. Then I answer a series of simple questions and take consistent and deliberate action based on my responses to those questions.

Step #1: Create an environment of financial abundance

Conventional personal finance wisdom says that you should "pay yourself first," meaning that you should put money aside in your savings before paying regular monthly bills. When it comes to manifesting money, there is a third step after paying yourself first and paying your regular bills second, which is to pay your creditors third. For example, manifesting money for a trip to Oahu when you've owed your parents $2,000 for over a year skips that part of the equation. You cannot expect the Universe to freely deliver money to you when you keep from others money that is owed to them. Therefore, to put myself in a money manifestation mindset, I make a list of the people to whom I owe money so that I can make sure I pay them before asking the Universe to pay me.

For example, if I want to manifest money to take a $300 French class, I first make sure that I am current on my payments to my book editor and publicity consultant. You can still manifest money if you have outstanding debts. Just make sure you have established a clear payment plan that both parties agree upon, and that you are current on those payments. If you are behind on payments or owe someone money, increase the amount of your ask (the amount of money you want to manifest) so that you can pay yourself first, pay your regular bills second, and pay your creditors next.

After paying my creditors, I create a physical environment of financial abundance by clearing my home office, purse, and email inbox of clutter. These are all portals through which I often receive money. By decluttering my living space, work space, purse, and email inbox, I am creating physical space and mental calm with which to accept the money I expect to receive. When decluttering, I often come across checks I've forgotten to cash (for shame!), an abundance of loose change, and old bills that need to be shredded. As you prepare to receive the money you want, deposit those checks, put those coins in a pretty jar, and shred or file that old paperwork. Creating physical and mental space tells the Universe that you are ready to accept more.

Step #2: Cultivate an attitude of gratitude

It's easy to focus on what you don't have or how much life will be better when you finally get what you want. However, being conscious of the many privileges you enjoy now elevates your thoughts, which helps you recognize the financial opportunities that are already in front of you. An attitude of gratitude focused on thanking God or the Universe for what you are about to receive rather than begging for what you want is more effective in bringing you what you want.

Write out a list of the various things you are already grateful for, regardless of whether they are related to money. Read the list out loud with enthusiasm, conviction, and a happy heart. Then add to your gratitude list what you expect to receive. Write out the statements as if you already have them and read them aloud with the joy you will have when it comes true.

Step #3: Get clear and specific

Now that you have made mental and physical space to receive your new money, you are ready to answer these questions:

1. How much money do I want?
Whether it is $500 or $5,000, pick an amount that you are excited about and can realistically imagine receiving. Remember, authentic belief is a crucial part of manifestation, so don't ask for a million dollars if you don't genuinely believe you can manifest it!

2. What will I use the money for?
By identifying a specific use for the money, you allow your mind to look for solutions to your end goal that may not involve money. For example, you may think you need to manifest $6,000 to rent an apartment in Paris for three months. By pinpointing the end goal of the money that you desire, you may realize that you can achieve your goal another way, such as through house-sitting or moving in with a host family.

3. When do I want the money by?
You can pick a date arbitrarily, but it's best to pick a date related to your end goal. For example, let's say you want to manifest money to go on a spring break trip with your friends. You set the date for one month before spring break so you have enough time to make plans to use your newly manifested moolah. Tying your target date to your end goal is helpful because it will motivate you to actively work toward them. Use the deadline-driven adrenaline rush to keep you motivated in working toward your goal.

4. What am I willing to enthusiastically give in exchange for this money?

Here is where you can get really creative. Brainstorm any idea that is legal, safe, and within your own moral boundaries. If you run your own business, you can bring in some cash by raising your prices, reaching out to current clients for referrals, or by offering a new package. If you have a traditional 9-5 job, you can ask for a raise or consider taking on a side gig.

I want you to brainstorm as many ideas as possible, but I don't want you to stress out about this part of the process. I've often been surprised to see that the money I manifest by my target date comes from a source outside of all the ideas I brainstormed. The brainstorming process is valuable because it puts you in a giving mindset rather than a taking mindset. When creating your list of ways you could make money, focus on the skills, talents, and resources you have and how you can genuinely be of service to others. Once you brainstorm a list (whether it includes three ideas or thirty), begin taking action on the ideas that are quickest to implement and the ones you are most excited to do.

Step #4: Take consistent, inspired action and keep the faith

Once I begin taking action, I do not fret about whether the money is coming or not. I continue to take consistent, inspired action until I have reached my goal. Not all of your ideas will work, and that's okay. During this part of the process, it's important to focus on persistence, staying positive in the face of setbacks, and thinking creatively.

On the occasions that I don't reach my goal of manifesting money by a certain deadline, it is almost always because I stop taking action before my chosen deadline or that I completely forget about the goal in the first place and only remember it weeks or months later! Similar to how we often forget our New Year's resolutions a few weeks after making them, I forget my money manifestation goals when I don't actively work to keep them at the forefront.

Step #5: Focus on feeling good

Once you have started to take consistent, inspired action, you want to make sure that you focus on feeling good. Ask yourself: How would I feel if I already had the money to do what I want to do? Whatever that feeling is—thrilled, calm, driven—put yourself in that mental state *while* you work toward your goal. By feeling good throughout the process of manifesting money (rather than feeling anxious, overwhelmed, or frantic), you bring the money to you that much more quickly. If you do start to get worried, don't beat yourself up for having negative thoughts. Recognize the thought like a passing cloud and then get back to your feel-great place.

Step #6: Let the money come

While an important part of manifesting money is taking consistent, inspired action, I don't believe that our human effort is what brings the money to us. I think that it is our *belief* that the money is coming that attracts it to us. Once you have done all the prior steps: cultivated an environment of financial abundance and gratitude, gained clarity, taken consistent, inspired action, and focused on feeling good, all that is left to do is get out of the way and let your money miracle happen.

KANEISHA CONFESSIONAL

In the months preceding the launch of this book, it was time to pay my publicity consultant. The price was $3,000 for our next engagement, which was a tremendous amount of money for me at the time. I had enough clients to cover my own living expenses for the next several months, but certainly not enough for this. Rather than panicking about losing my publicist or using my money for my living expenses to pay her (remember, we pay creditors third), I decided to manifest the money.

"Three thousand dollars is a lot of money for me, but I think your work is worth it and I want to be able to pay you. I am going to do my best to manifest the money by Friday," I told her on Monday of that week. "If I manifest the money by Friday, we're on. If I don't, I'll have to say goodbye."

Once we hung up, I made a list of several ways I could manifest $3,000 in four days. Once I had my list, I took immediate action. First, I created a twenty-four-hour sale, spotlighting my most popular admissions consulting package at a discounted rate of $1,000. I immediately emailed my mailing list with the offer, fully expecting at least three people to take the bait. Not one person did. Rather than getting discouraged or frantically taking more action, I focused on feeling how I would feel when I received the $3,000 I wanted: happy and calm.

The same night, I received an application for my premium one-on-one admissions consulting package. I had one coaching spot left, and had recently considered closing the door to new clients with the empty spot left open. Thank God I didn't! I was elated to see that the prospective client indicated she was interested in my largest package, which was $15,000. We set up a call for the next day to discuss the possibility of working together. We had a great call, and at the end, I asked if she would be able to make a $3,000 deposit by Friday. "Oh, I can make it by Wednesday," she quipped. My heart sang. I had manifested the $3,000 I needed to pay my publicist within forty-eight hours and was going to end up earning even more than the original amount I had hoped for.

When my new client sent me the $3,000 the next day, I truly felt like I had experienced a money miracle. It was one of the largest and quickest money manifestations of my life. From that day on, I knew that I possessed a power that would serve me the rest of my life. I also realized I needed to share it with others. Go forth and manifest your own money miracle!

Chapter 12:
Remember to "Do You"

Don't be satisfied with stories,
how things have gone with others.
Unfold your own myth.
— RUMI

As I MENTIONED BEFORE, I'm a bit of a self-help junkie. At one point in my life, I devoured personal development books as fast as I could get my hands on them. I felt like I was unlocking the secrets to the Universe in books like, well, *The Secret*. I felt compelled to keep reading to ensure I wouldn't miss out on some life-changing "get the real deal" inside scoop on how to live a great life. Eventually, I mellowed out on my exclusively self-help diet and found my way back to reading a mix of tantalizing fiction, business, and motivational books. My dive into the world of "you can do it!" taught me that yes, I can do it, but I don't need to do *everything* to be happy. In fact, rather than trying to buff all my rough edges away, I realized I was better off focusing my time and attention on what matters most to me rather than trying to win life's all-around most improved award. Instead, I realized I wanted to master a few key things in life—and have a lot of fun doing it. In short, I started to redefine my definition of success, and in turn, started thinking about my life in a completely different way.

What It Means to Be Successful

At some point in life—likely during the middle school years—we "smart girls" stop passionately talking about what we want to be when we grow up, and we start focusing on how to catch the attention of the boys, gain approval from our teachers, and win acceptance from the cool kids. This obsession with external validation continues throughout high school and then into college, where we continue to balance puppy love pining, social jockeying, and academic grinding. Then around senior year of college, we start to think about life in the real world (or in my case, how we can put off the real world a little bit longer by going to graduate school). By then, many of us have long stowed away our dreams of taking over the world while doing what we love and have replaced our ambitions with the vague but persistent notion that we must be above all else "successful."

As an admissions consultant and self-help writer, I have worked with and counseled hundreds of young people hungrily chasing an elusive idea of success. I myself have been that young person and still am in many ways. However, an experience I had one Saturday afternoon opened my eyes to the true meaning of success. It helped me realize that success isn't a title bestowed upon you from the outside; it's a personal journey that only you can define.

KANEISHA CONFESSIONAL

One weekend, I accompanied my friend Adia to shop for some vintage, midcentury rosewood furniture. (This is the type of furniture you would see on the TV show Mad Men.*) Rosewood is extremely durable and lustrous, making it ideal for furniture and musical instruments like the guitar. The seller's two-car garage was wide open, revealing countless rosewood tables, chairs, and desks packed tightly and carefully like perfectly placed Tetris blocks.*

As Adia and I pulled up to the Craigslist seller's home, we both gasped and whispered to one another, taking turns guessing at the chaotically organized spectacle before us.

"Oh my goodness, he's a hoarder!" I breathed.

"Or maybe the hoarder died and this poor guy is selling all his stuff . . . " Adia ventured.

Adia and I quickly learned that the Craigslist vendor was not, in fact, a hoarder. His family specialized in buying, restoring, and reselling midcentury rosewood furniture, and they stored their inventory in the garage of their home. The seller knew how to quickly find and deftly extricate every single piece of furniture in that garage without leaving a ding or scratch.

During the brief time we spent with the rosewood expert, I watched him work in slack-jawed awe. He knew about the history of rosewood, how to best clean and affordably store it, how to buy it cheaply and then resell it for premium prices. He also had a good sense of when it was worth his time to fix up pieces to sell at premium prices and when it was better for him to offload it on Craigslist at a low price. Typically, his Craigslist buyers knew the value of rosewood furniture and were happy to pay his well-informed asking prices.

"You are a master of midcentury rosewood furniture," I murmured as I watched him use a tiny ball of steel wool to gently scrub flecks of paint from the legs of a chair, leaving not a single scratch.

"Of course I am," he said nonchalantly. "This is what my parents did, and it's what I do, too. This is natural to me."

The rosewood man knew everything there was to know about midcentury rosewood furniture. His face emanated joy and pride as he effortlessly packed Adia's Jeep with a five-foot long dining table and six chairs. In the half hour we spent at his home, the rosewood man sold more than $1,000 worth of furniture to Adia and other rosewood appreciators.

Visibly enjoying my awe and admiration, the rosewood man pulled out a stack of invoices and proudly showed me the dozens of orders he receives every month for his pieces. Half dazed, I smiled and congratulated him as I scanned the invoices, littered with dollar signs and zeros. Not only was he a master at his craft; he was being paid well for it too!

That afternoon, I realized what it meant to be successful.

SELF-LOVE PRINCIPLE #34

Success is mastering something that matters to you.

Before that weekend, I had no idea what midcentury rosewood furniture was or that people paid thousands of dollars for it even when used. Even after that experience, I knew I would most likely go back to my old habit of furnishing my place with hand-me-downs and Ikea pieces. Midcentury rosewood furniture just doesn't matter to me.

But it mattered to the rosewood man and his customers around the world. To the benefit of himself, his family, and his customers, he had mastered the art of preserving and selling rosewood. This craft was his art. There was no doubt in my mind that he was successful.

A SELF-LOVE STORY

Before I got married and had my son, I was focused on the world's definition of what success looked like: going to good schools, having nice jobs, being very smart and ambitious, and making sure that I could display my successes to the world. But after I had my son, a lot of that became less important. It made me reevaluate what really makes me happy, what really motivates me and drives my passion. A lot of that is just helping people, especially helping children.

— 29 years old, Atlanta, GA, married

While rosewood isn't my thing, I gain clarity each and every day on what I want to do with my life. I aim to master the art of teaching and inspiring myself and others through words and ideas, especially through sharing my own experiences and insights. That's why I love writing, coaching, and reading personal development books. Gaining clarity in my definition of success has helped me focus on my goals and given meaning to many activities that, to outsiders, could seem like hobbies. Blogging and social media marketing aren't just fun ways for me to be creative; they are exercises in mastery. Doing these things consistently and learning how to improve moves me closer to my goal of mastering the art of influence and inspiration.

Whether you want to master the art of parenting, skiing, painting, sales, hairdressing, or luscious living, take the time to think about what matters most to you. If you dedicate the time and effort to truly mastering something meaningful to you, you will inevitably be successful. Even if it isn't your full-time job, the payoff comes in the form of knowing that you didn't squander your talents on mediocre effort. The payoff is in knowing you gave your best to something and, in turn, enjoyed the satisfaction of knowing there is something in this world to which you dedicated your heart and soul.

Why You Don't Need to Be Well-Rounded

It seems like everywhere you look, society is constantly urging young people to be well-rounded. We feel the pressure to be smart, athletic, artistic, musical, and highly social. However, when you look at people who make history—the thought leaders, social change agents, and legacy-creating individuals—they were not necessarily well-rounded people. Consider Albert Einstein, Alice Walker, Michael Jackson, Mahatma Gandhi, Amelia Earhart, and of course, let's not forget Beyoncé Carter! They identified their passions and talents, shared that gift with the world, and became increasingly skilled and influential through the sharing and mastery of that gift.

Truly great people have a laser focus on what they really love and share their gifts no matter how small the audience. They don't seek to be well-rounded or, in other words, a "little bit good" at everything. They seek to be outstanding at what they do. They offset a relentless drive to share their ever-unfolding gifts with a sense of balance in their lives.

Balance is different from well-roundedness. Balance means that all your time, energy, and money is not going into one place. For example, a great musician spends many hours a day playing music, but she also spends time with her family and friends, working out, and meditating. If all she did was stay cooped up in the studio playing music, where would she get the inspiration to feed her work? It's important to take time away from that special gift to make time for other things that bring joy and calm. A balanced life gives you somewhere to go—not to escape the challenges and rewards brought on by being great—but to replenish your mind, body, and spirit so you can continue to be great.

But what if you really are quite good at a lot of different things? The pitfall of being well-rounded is that you could end up succumbing to a wandering sense of obligation. This is the gifted painter who suffers through an economics class in college not because she is curious about the topic, but because she feels like she's "supposed to." Diversity in one's interests and passions can be helpful in bringing new perspectives and approaches to a situation. However, these diverse interests and passions should organically emerge in the process of pursuing what you really want to do.

Introspection is important to evolving as a person, but don't put too much focus on improving your weaknesses. Find the opportunities where you shine. Once you discover your gift, abandon well-roundedness for the pursuit of mastering and sharing that gift with the world.

SELF-LOVE PRINCIPLE #35
All people have a God-given gift that, if nurtured, would blossom tremendously and change lives. Invest in nurturing and expressing your gift.

Why Not You?

One sunny afternoon while I was living well above my means in Santa Monica, my friend Lori came over to my apartment for lunch. I began telling her about my decision to focus more on my goals of being a writer rather than spending and acting as if I were rich, as I had been doing for the past year since I graduated. Lori listened intently and enthusiastically to my decision to realign my spending habits with my professional goals. She later emailed me a video highlighting the story of then twenty-six-year-old writer Amanda Hocking, who spent years writing and self-publishing a shocking seventeen books while working a full-time job. When I first learned about her, she had recently become wildly successful with her low-priced e-books for young adults as the craze for vampire and werewolf fiction reached its peak. Amanda has since secured a multimillion-dollar publishing deal and writes full-time. I was filled with inspiration and glee as I watched the video.

I love Amanda's story of being a self-publishing success because at the time her books exploded, she was a "normal" person with no special connections. All she did was write her vampire-loving butt off! According to interviews, she never imagined herself ever doing anything else as a profession. She wrote unceasingly even though she faced consistent rejection from traditional publishers. She wrote with conviction and purpose, and now she is reaping the financial and spiritual rewards of persistently doing what she loved to do. That is awesome!

I revel in stories of people who are living their dreams after years of perseverance. Rather than sulk and think, *Oh, well, they're different from me because of this and that,* I just soak up all the goodness emanating from their stories and envision success happening in my own life.

BYOB BROSPECTIVE

The biggest piece of advice that I've gotten from my mentor is "Do you." The reason he gave me that advice is because over the years, I've been saying all these different things like: "I know that I'm talented in X and Y, but no one's really responding. I see this person having this amount of success. This person has X number of Twitter followers, X number of Facebook fans." And my mentor replied, "Slim, stop worrying about all the other stuff that's going around you and just focus on doing you. Your path is your path. Your journey is your journey, and you'll arrive right on time."

— Slim Jackson, personal development blogger at TheRealSlimJackson.com, lifestyle blogger at SingleBlackMale.org

All too often, when we encounter a story of someone who has "made it"—whether she got a big promotion, married her perfect partner, or earned a fancy award—our first reaction is to dismiss the possibility of such a lovely thing happening in our own life.

You think: *That winner, that woman getting what she always wanted, is not like me. She has more money, more time, more friends, more connections, more ideas, less debt, fewer worries, and weighs less than me. She's just had an easy life, and really, it isn't even fair that she's winning right now.* But that line of thinking is irrational, self-destructive, and 100 percent untrue. For all you know, that successful woman that you think has had it so easy has an alcoholic dad, an undiagnosed learning disorder, an embarrassing phobia of heights, and flat feet. She failed kindergarten, had no friends in middle school, and still owes back taxes from a business that floundered. Even if you don't know the details, be sure to know that girl's got problems just like the rest of us. But she did get what she wanted in a few areas of her life. And if it looks like something that you want, don't focus on trying to minimize her success. Believe that it can be yours too. As my mom would say, "Quit hating, and start elevating."

The next time you find a shining example of something you want, put down that chilled glass of strawberry-flavored haterade and enjoy basking in someone else's success. Then take a moment to tell yourself that you too can have that.

SELF-LOVE PRINCIPLE #36
**When you learn of someone else's success,
don't hate—celebrate!
There's enough success to go around!**

Chapter 13:
You Can Do It,
Put Your Best into It

Doing the best at this moment
puts you in the best place for the next moment.
— OPRAH WINFREY

AT THIS POINT, you may be feeling overwhelmed with all the advice, ideas, suggestions, and lists. You may feel motivated to change your life but you're wondering where to start. Should you journal about it? Meditate on it? Talk about it with your friends, a mentor, a coach? My suggestion is to pick something you want in your life— be it a new job, the ability to live a certain lifestyle, or getting in better shape—and just get started. Do your best, and let the Universe take care of the rest.

Get Your Hands Dirty

Even when we have a clear idea of what we want to do in life, we often find ourselves paralyzed from taking action to actually achieve the goals we have articulated. It's easy to keep yourself occupied in pursuits tangentially related to your interests without producing tangible results that move you closer to your goals. When your focus is more on planning than actually *doing*, you can easily end up spinning your wheels for years—or for a lifetime.

KANEISHA CONFESSIONAL

I spent an entire year fixated (though not focused) on the idea of being a self-help writer, talk show hostess, and filmmaker. I made some progress in getting closer to my writing goal by launching a blog, writing regularly for Harvard's student-run newspaper, and writing a book proposal.

On the other hand, in all of my planning for the future, I passed up a lot of hands-on opportunities that may have pushed me closer to my goals. I thought that instead of jumping into the world of media and entertainment as an unpaid intern, I could network and charm my way in. My thinking was, I have two master's degrees from Harvard. Why should I be filing mail in the basement of a talent agency?

However, after merely four weeks of aimless "networking" in Los Angeles, I realized the value of actually getting your hands dirty working in the industry—even in a "lowly" position.

While networking is an essential skill to exercise in a relationship-driven industry like media and entertainment, you also have to be willing to actually create something of value that people can react to and evaluate. An inspiring coffee chat with a fellow alumnus from Pomona College now working as a television writer inspired me to channel the energy I was putting into networking into actually creating something. That way, when I showed up to a meeting, I wasn't just smiling blankly and asking questions; I had something to show. Once I sat down and decided to write my book rather than spend months shopping around a proposal for an unwritten book, I found so many more opportunities opening up for me. I finally realized that I needed to stop thinking and talking about what I was going to do and actually do it!

If you're like me, it's easy to talk ad nauseam about your hopes and dreams without making any real progress. I know it seems obvious, but getting your hands dirty doing what you say you want to do is the best way to determine if you are indeed cut out for that line of work.

Here are two ways to stop talking and start getting your hands dirty:

1. Take advantage of time-sensitive opportunities.
For those of you still in college or graduate school, consider yourself lucky. High-profile, time-crunched alumni tend to be more open to having informational interviews with you. Companies are willing to take you on as an intern. And the money you have from your student loans or scholarships sometimes make money less of an urgent obligation. If you are a student, use your summers and for-credit learning opportunities such as field studies, research projects, and independent study projects to explore working in the

field you are passionate about joining. Even if the day-to-day work is not exactly what you hope to be doing full-time, you will often make valuable connections and be promoted to more meaningful and relevant work after having proven yourself.

During the short time that I pursued a career in media and entertainment, I did an unpaid for-credit internship for Overbrook Entertainment, Will Smith's production company. Even though the company did not ultimately offer me a paid full-time position, I learned a lot about the industry and made some valuable connections. You better believe that once I'm ready to pitch the movie adaptation of *Be Your Own Boyfriend*, the contacts I made there will be the first people I call!

Be honest about what you want to do when someone asks, "What do you want to be when you grow up?" If you really want to be a fine artist, don't tell people you want to be a lawyer. While it may feel better to tell people what they want to hear or give the socially acceptable answer, being dishonest with yourself and others about your dreams is a disservice to you. You miss out on the opportunity to craft your own destiny if you don't confidently claim your dreams. You also miss the very real opportunity to meet someone with information or a connection that can help you get closer to your dream. You never know where your big break might come from. Let folks know who you really are and what you really want in life.

As the old adage goes, "It is better to be hated for who you are than loved for who you aren't." Sometimes, I can get a bit self-conscious letting people know that I am a coach and writer and that I'd like to have my own talk show one day. Depending on what city I'm in, people can be dismissive of what they see as a "woo woo" job or a self-absorbed career goal. However, I know that I mustn't apologize or silence myself to gain approval from others. Everyone has a dream, and that's mine!

2. Start today.

Rather than aiming to have all the details perfectly in place, begin engaging as both an observer and creator within the field you want to be in. It's okay if everything you create isn't of the highest quality in the early stages. In the first few years of my blog, my readers saw my site go through a dizzying array of different looks as I learned more about coding and graphic design. Instead of getting paralyzed from starting because my blog didn't look perfect, I kept writing with the hope that people would be lured into the site by its compelling content. As my income and technical skills increased, so did the quality of my site's design. However, at that point, I'm not sure how much a pretty website mattered. Since I had already established a consistent publishing schedule, my fans were more interested in what I had to say rather than how cute my website was.

The importance of getting your hands dirty seems like common sense, but sometimes those of us with the most formal education are the most reluctant to roll up our sleeves and get our hands dirty. We are used to striving for perfection—in a safe classroom setting where there are grades and "rules" for success. As my friend Kobina, a documentary filmmaker, often says, "Strive for excellence rather than perfection," so you can finally get started working toward your dreams.

SELF-LOVE PRINCIPLE #37
**Pursue your career goals with persistence
regardless of what other people say, think, or do.**

Always Do Your Best

As you start getting down and dirty working on achieving your goals, it's important to remember that you don't have to do things perfectly. You just have to do your best. It's a simple but powerful lesson that I carry with me.

KANEISHA CONFESSIONAL

One day when I was still living in Santa Monica, I arrived at my friend Laura's house, excited to spend time with one of my most ambitious, creative friends. Laura is the successful Internet entrepreneur that I mention earlier in this book, and I take her advice seriously. She had just finished reading a tiny book called The Four Agreements. *"I think you should read it," she said. "I bet you'll really like it."*

Frankly, it looked like a young adult book to me, being so tiny with a colorful cover. Many months later, I remembered Laura's suggestion and wandered into an Austin bookstore. I asked an employee for the book, calling it "a spiritual book called The Four Somethings," *and the clerk immediately knew which book I was referring to. I purchased two copies—one for myself and one for my mom, who was spending the weekend with me in Plano, Texas for my much-anticipated television audition for the Oprah Winfrey Network (OWN).*

My mother and I finished the book over two days and loved it. One of the main lessons of the book was the chapter titled "Always Do Your Best." If you always do your best, author Don Miguel Ruiz writes, you free yourself from regret and self-doubt. After all, if you do your best, what more can you or anyone else ask for?

This was the perfect book for me to read the night before my big audition. The Four Agreements emboldened me to give my all to the audition. I practiced my introduction, made sure I looked my best, and sat cheerfully and calmly at the table with the other aspiring hosts. I did well in the first round of auditions and was called back for an on-camera audition the next day. For both auditions, I did my very best. I was relaxed, confident, and radiated positive energy as I delivered my pitch for my very own talk show. I felt exhilarated after both auditions. No matter what happened, I had been the best Kaneisha I could be. I would have no regrets and no what-ifs.

I didn't end up moving past the second-round audition, but I didn't beat myself up about it or sulk (well, not that much) because I had done my very best. I never received any feedback, so I'm not sure why I wasn't chosen. In my mind, it just wasn't my time.

This experience of doing my very best prompted me to reflect upon the many times when I have put forth a bare minimum amount of effort or none at all. Yes, I'm a very accomplished person, but how much richer might my life be if I did my best at everything I took on rather than doing a good enough job to get by? What would your life look like if you did your best? I bet if you committed to doing your best at all times, you'd quickly get clear on what *really* mattered to you and focus your energy there.

Always doing your best is not about ceaselessly striving for something more and better. It's not about being a perfectionist or endlessly competing with yourself. It's about meeting each experience, challenge, and opportunity with your best self. Rather than avoiding the problem, fearing a challenge, or clinging to a potential outcome, take a deep breath, do your best, and move on.

Always doing your best might sound exhausting, but it's exactly the opposite. Doing your best and having no regrets is energizing and affirming. You may surprise yourself with what you are capable of. When you do your best, you put yourself in a position to be enormously grateful, divinely inspired, and encouraging to others. You find that the outer limits of "your best" begin to expand, like a swimmer who, with each consecutive practice, is able to swim a farther distance without coming up for a breath. Your best becomes bigger and better than you thought possible.

SELF-LOVE PRINCIPLE #38
By always doing your best, you can focus on the journey rather than worry about the outcome of your efforts.

Be Willing to Do That Which Makes Your Eyes Bleed

Among my girlfriends at Harvard, I was often outspoken about the many situations and tasks that—as I loved to say—"make my eyes bleed." I'm talking about the tedious to-dos and errands involved in reaching my goals, the things you wish a little gnome would just magically appear and do for you. However, I recently discovered the one characteristic that sets apart the people who accomplish their goals and dreams from the people who merely talk about them. This differentiating characteristic is a willingness to do that which makes their eyes bleed. At minimum, successful people are willing to do the bleeding-eye-inducing tasks that bring them closer to their goals and dreams.

It's easy to be enthusiastic and diligent about working toward your dreams when all the projects are new and exciting. However, there will come a time when the project is no longer novel and fun, and only the monotonous, mind-numbing tasks lie ahead. Marketing guru Seth Godin refers to this trying time as "The Dip" in his aptly titled book *The Dip*. Unfortunately, The Dip often comes at the same time as a slowdown in income, attention, resources, or some other game-changing challenge. It's a deadly combination: the end of the initial burst of enthusiasm and an unexpected scarcity of resources. It happens all the time.

The Dip is where most "big idea" people give up. They think, *I started this because I thought it would be fun. It's my passion. But this stuff here in front of me isn't fun anymore. It's kind of tedious. And hard. I might as well quit now before this bankrupts me or bores me to death.*

What Seth teaches us, however, is that those who make it through The Dip's treacherous wasteland emerge on the other side, leading the pack because they persevered while others gave up prematurely or got distracted by a shiny, new project. Yes, sometimes it is the right decision to give up. However, all too often, we give up just as the breakthrough is on the horizon.

BYOB BROSPECTIVE

A lot of people talk about the concepts of hard work and talent. But one thing people underestimate is the power of discipline. There was a point where I was a serial project starter. Even up until six months ago, every week I had a new idea, a new project, or some new movement I wanted to start. So it went from, "Oh I want to write a book," to, "Oh I want to start this health movement," to, "Oh I want to have this personal development megablog," to, "Oh I want to change careers and do this," to, "Oh I want to run track." And for me, it really got to a point where I realized that I couldn't have success— or the type of success that I would like—by doing ten different things. I really needed to focus on one or two things.

— Slim Jackson, personal development blogger at
TheRealSlimJackson.com, lifestyle blogger at SingleBlackMale.org

It's difficult to anticipate the tasks that will make your eyes bleed, but you will recognize them when they come by the sheer amount of Resistance you will encounter when it's time to get down to work.

SELF-LOVE PRINCIPLE #39
**The willingness to identify what needs to be done,
create a plan, and then execute that plan
—even when it's not fun—will drive you to success.**

Every project—no matter how fun it is—is going to have some annoying elements that make your eyes bleed. Here are a few examples of the mundane tasks I must do as a writer, coach, and business owner:

- **Keep track of receipts for taxes.** It's not hard to do, but it is just plain annoying holding on to every little piece of paper that shows I bought paper clips for my home office or a cappuccino for a client.

- **Draft and review contracts.** This is an essential part of my business yet every single time, I'm tempted to just skip this part and go straight to working together. Spelling out every little scenario that might happen makes me want to howl at the moon in agonized boredom, but I also understand that contracts are important to protecting both of our interests.

- **Fill out, scan, and send speaker agreements and freelance writing invoices.** I know it sounds crazy, but I'm often tempted to just not even send these in. Yes, it means I won't get paid but it also means I won't have to do the paperwork!

- **Wait for videos to be converted to the right file format and uploaded to YouTube.** Why, sweet baby Buddha does it take so long to get a video from my Macbook to the

Internet? I can't wait for Internet that works faster than our brains (which may already be the case) because right now, this part of my business is making my brain hurt.

And the list goes on. In order for my business to operate and my career to progress, this work must get done. It took me several years of being out of graduate school in the "real world" to understand that no matter what career path you choose, there will be times of boredom, tedium, and eye-bleeding tasks. However, when you pursue a career that feeds your passion and plays to your strengths, it's worth the pain.

Even when your career is based on your passion, there will be many times when your eyes will bleed. For example, creative expression and teaching others matters a lot to me. Being a writer and coach is the culmination of two of my most powerful motivators. It's like a Kaneisha Motivation Cocktail on the rocks. Sounds great, right? How could I not love every moment of following my dreams and being my own boss? But as evidenced from my earlier list, there are many tasks I must do to maintain my business and advance my career that make my eyes bleed. And my head hurt. And my face itch.

However, I know that if I can push through and consistently deliver outstanding content, products, and services to the people who have granted me their trust and attention, it will all be worth it. So as I sit here crouched over my laptop, eyes slowly bleeding (I really didn't feel like writing tonight), I urge you to stick with a project when it's no longer super fun or sexy. Instead, focus on finding something for which you are willing to push through the boredom to the other side, where the rewards of persistence and perseverance lie waiting for you.

Without Purse or Script, Go

What are the mental messages you replay that list all the reasons you cannot pursue your dreams today—or ever?

- I don't have the resources to succeed.

- I don't have enough money to start a business.

- I'm not ready to write that novel.

- I don't have the time or talent to paint that image I have in my mind.

Know this: you already have everything you need to succeed in achieving your dreams. "Without purse or script" is a phrase from the biblical story where Jesus orders his apostles to evangelize and serve the world without clear directions or guaranteed resources. I first heard the phrase when I was sitting in service at the Agape International Spiritual Center in California. I loved it as soon as I heard it.

The "purse" refers to any limited resource you would ordinarily think is vital to your success. For most people, this is money. I firmly believe that if you "follow your bliss," as the late mythologist Joseph Campbell advised us, all of your needs will eventually be met. Experiencing success by faithfully following my dreams has been the story of my life up to this point, and I cannot wait to see how it plays out over the next few years.

Traveling "without purse" means not allowing money—whether you have it or you don't—to be a hurdle to pursuing your dreams. Some people feel like they don't have enough money to start. Other people have plenty of money and fear losing it if they try something new and risky. Money can always be an excuse, but it never should be because it is entirely replaceable one way or another.

I think of the term "script" in two ways: (1) as a roadmap telling you where to go and which steps to take, and (2) as the scripted conventional wisdom we often hear repeated throughout our lives. Scripts are ideas created by other people that we then repeat to ourselves and make our own truth, just as an actor might memorize lines for a movie. Scripts are assumptions and beliefs that we have inherited from other people. The scripts we inherit from other people are often not even original; they may just be passing the scripts on from someone else far removed and irrelevant to you. How crazy is that: to be living your life according to some disconnected notion of how things should be, advice that may have nothing to do with your life!

In pursuing your dreams, there will never be a clear-cut, guaranteed path to success. Nor is success guaranteed. Let's say your dream is to be an actor. You could do all the things you are "supposed" to do—get stunning headshots, audition persistently for parts, act in small productions—and you still may not become a movie star. Los Angeles is full of people who tried out acting and eventually decided that other dreams deserved their time and attention. So it's true; you won't always get what you want when you want it the way you want it. However, the path to your dreams has to start somewhere, which is right where you are at this moment. Take a step.

The second kind of script includes the so-called truisms that we let stand in the way of our dreams. These truisms are usually based on half-truths, unfounded "facts," or misinformation. They closely resemble the self-limiting talk I mention earlier. The kinds of self-defeating scripts I often played in my mind when I was first embarking on my career as a writer and entrepreneur were

- *I can't be self-employed. Then I won't have health insurance and I won't be able to pay back my student loans!*

- *Who am I to think that I can just jump into working for myself? I should take some baby steps first and then eventually do what I really want to do.*

- *No writer ever makes enough money to actually live. I'll end up a poor, lonely loser without a "real" job.*

Whenever a script starts sabotaging my resolve to pursue my dreams, I make a point to write it down so that I can acknowledge, name, and confront the fear. Unearthing the fearful assumption gives me clarity in being able to test the idea by gathering more information. After unearthing and investigating the assumptions I had about self-employment, I realized that I could indeed find affordable health insurance as a self-employed person. I learned that some writers *do* make enough money to support themselves through their writing. Of course, many others write while keeping their day jobs, and that isn't the end of the world either if it means they are pursuing their dreams. When I confronted my particular scripts related to working for myself, I had no excuses left, and it was a wonderful feeling. I now live my life moving toward my dreams without purse or script. Please join me!

A SELF-LOVE STORY

There was a time when my friend and BYOB Expert Arielle Loren felt stifled at her 9-5 job and yearned to pursue her passion of enhancing the global dialogue about sex. So what did she do? She launched *CORSET* magazine and moved to Brazil. Now she lives the life of travel and creativity that she always dreamed of, and in just a few weeks from the time that I am writing this, she will be joining me in my hometown of Austin to copresent a talk at the prestigious and fun megaconference South by Southwest. Here's what Arielle has to say about boldly going after your dreams:

I think people underestimate how much they can really do if they just put their minds to it. And then some of it is just serendipity. When you make a decision and it sits well with your gut, and it's something that your intuition is telling you to do, usually, there are cards being played that you can't see yet. They are going to help you along the way. You just have to trust the process.

Whatever your dreams are for your career or your life, know that there will always be a million reasons not to go for it, not to start, and not to try. The key is to remember that there will never be a foolproof path to success. Without purse or script, just go!

SELF-LOVE PRINCIPLE #40

You are the person, the permission, the right time, and the sign you have been waiting for.

Conclusion

Life begins at the end of your comfort zone.
— NEALE DONALD WALSCH

GET IT, GIRL! You have now discovered the strategies, tips, and self-love principles to begin the lifelong journey of being your own boyfriend. No matter what your relationship status is, you now have a toolbox for living a joyful life of laughter, friendship, adventure, achievement, release, and abundant love, knowing that the most important relationship is the one you have with yourself.

In Part One, you unearthed the sinister threats to your happiness. Whether it's comparing yourself to other people (never!) or limiting yourself in the words you choose, these threats can no longer rule your life or steal your joy. You also learned how to let go of old relationships and men who can't give you what you want.

In Part Two, you kicked the lid off your sexy can and let your sensuality loose! You learned why sexiness matters, and you reminded yourself of the real target of your sex appeal. (Take a look in the mirror, girl!) You picked up some easy ways to boost your va-va-voom factor while still being the same lovable you. You discovered the ultimate secrets to sensual single living and have now joined the worldwide league of luscious women who get their daily O in and out of the bedroom.

In Part Three, you took a step back to see yourself clearly. You devoted time to nurture your passions, reflected on what you really wanted, and faced what was holding you back. You began to practice the power of gracefully saying no, freeing you up to say *yes!* to what really matters to you. You vowed to attract happiness and calm into your life by leaving the drama on the stage where it rightly belongs. You got the wake-up call to stop merely telling people your plans and actually start *doing* what you really want to do. Most importantly, you learned that you can have a dream without a surefire plan and that taking action is the way the divine plan will be revealed to you.

I hope that you realize by now that being your own boyfriend is not about dating or not dating. It's about the power of courting yourself for the rest of your life, getting to know yourself better every day, and falling in love with yourself and your life over and over again.

Now that you've discovered the secret of being your own boyfriend, go out and find support to stay on this path. You can start a *Be Your Own Boyfriend* Accountability Group, a supportive sisterhood of empowered women who come together to share their struggles and successes with being their own boyfriends. A mix of fun events, girl talks, and learning opportunities could help you make new friends, move closer to your goals, and spread the BYOB movement. (Self-defense lessons followed by cocktails and tapas, anyone? Sounds like a great time to me!)

Now that you are in the BYOB tribe, share this book with any friend or acquaintance you think could benefit from the message. Be warned: some people will smirk or scoff when you tell them about a book you read titled *Be Your Own Boyfriend*. When I tell people about my book, I have encountered every reaction you can imagine. One guy I met at a bar laughed sardonically and told me that having written a book with that title, I will be single forever. (Believe it or not, this very same guy was one of the first people to buy a copy of the book as soon as it was available for pre-order! That just goes to show that those who seem like your critics are sometimes just putting on a front to disguise rabid curiosity!) Despite the random haters and cynics, most people are excited to learn such an easy-to-remember self-love sound bite. Even if your friends and family don't share your BYOB enthusiasm, remember that you now know the secrets to happiness, sexiness, and getting what you want. You have the power to change your life—regardless of what other people say, think, or do.

Basically, I want you to share the delicious secrets of *Be Your Own Boyfriend* in whatever way feels most fun and natural to you. Blog about your own journey being your own boyfriend. Tweet your favorite quotes from the book. Create a Pinterest board or Instagram account featuring you getting your daily experiential orgasm. (I'll say it again: show yourself getting your *experiential* O, not the physical one!) Lend your copy of *Be Your Own Boyfriend* to your best girlfriend—or better yet, buy her a copy as a surprise. Many, though not all, of your girlfriends will be grateful that you nudged them in the direction of claiming their lives now rather than wasting precious time waiting for a man to complete them or fix their lives.

In case you're wondering how my self-love journey is going, I'm still working on it just like you. I'm continuously practicing the fine art of making my health, happiness, and peace of mind my top priority. Believe me, it hasn't been easy. Deep down, I'm still the same boy crazy Kaneisha that has to remind herself to stay centered and balanced in the wake of a new relationship.

If you're also wondering whether penning a book titled *Be Your Own Boyfriend* scared all the good men away, let me assure you it has done exactly the opposite. In the past year in particular, I had to fight the men off with a stick! It seems that telling men that you are "being your own boyfriend" only makes them want to prove you wrong and earn the title of boyfriend (and sometimes I let them try . . .). During the time since I've moved back to Austin, I have dated a variety of interesting, smart, gorgeous men—Black, White, Indian, Latino, Asian, and always smart and sexy. Though I went on many fun dates and even became exclusive with several guys, none of my Austin suitors have turned out to be The One—at least not yet.

I'll admit it: meeting so many new men in the last year has been bittersweet. When relationships don't work out, there's always a pang of sadness—and sometimes lots of tears—from my grief of what could've been if only we were compatible. Unlike with my old D.C. debacle, I now have the strength, wisdom, and clarity to let go of a relationship when I realize it's not working. With every guy I've dated since then, I ended the relationship with love and respect. There is not one guy who would make me want to duck behind the nearest oak tree if I were to see him out in public. (We all have that one "oak tree" guy that we acted a straight up fool with, don't we?) Writing, revising, and living the mantra of being my own boyfriend has helped me date with integrity and dignity. It has helped me to honor myself and what I want. Dating is no longer a burden or a complicated game of relationship chess. These days, it's easier, more enjoyable, and more of an adventure.

I am still looking forward to meeting and spending the rest of my life with a partner. In the meantime, I am finding a wonderful companion in myself, and our relationship gets better each day. After so many years of chasing after men to make me feel whole, I am in love with myself and my life, crazy times and all. I still email out *The Love Note* every week, and my community of self-loving mavens has grown from a few hundred when I first started to more than 1,400 people at the time of printing this book. I can't wait for our self-loving tribe to grow to 14,000, then 140,000+ women and men dedicated to learning how to build the life of their dreams and being their own best friends.

Go ahead and jump headfirst into being your own boyfriend. Love yourself unapologetically, and let the world see how much you really mean it. When people see how you radiate joy and confidence, they will have no choice but to examine their own souls in search of the golden happiness you have uncovered. Your commitment to love yourself out loud won't change your life alone. Indeed, it can change the world.

Love,
Kaneisha

Appendix

Self-Love Principles

SELF-LOVE PRINCIPLE #1
**Real happiness comes from within
and is not based on the status of your romantic relationship.**

SELF-LOVE PRINCIPLE #2
**If you want others to love, appreciate, and respect you,
you must love, appreciate, and respect yourself first.**

SELF-LOVE PRINCIPLE #3
**Listen to what your mind, body, and spirit are telling you
about your happiness or lack thereof.
Once you start listening and stop ignoring,
you can start reclaiming your joy, health, and peace of mind.**

SELF-LOVE PRINCIPLE #4
**When you are your own biggest fan, other people's
opinions about your life matter far less.**

SELF-LOVE PRINCIPLE #5

You have the power to validate your own
feelings, thoughts, experiences, and accomplishments.
Your life is unique and can't be compared to anyone else's.

SELF-LOVE PRINCIPLE #6

Anything that you pay attention to has the power
to influence your thoughts, your feelings, and your life.
Feed your mind, body, and soul with inspiration and positivity.

SELF-LOVE PRINCIPLE #7

Use the power of your words to make your world
an abundant place of possibility.

SELF-LOVE PRINCIPLE #8

Release expectations for how your life "should be"
and be grateful for the blessings you have in your life
right now.

SELF-LOVE PRINCIPLE #9

Happiness is not the absence of problems.
It's about choosing which types of problems you want
and feeling empowered to accept and address them.

SELF-LOVE PRINCIPLE #10

Trying to please everyone is impossible and
undermines the power of your own inner compass.

SELF-LOVE PRINCIPLE #11

Do your best to solve your problems and then
trust that the Universe will take you the rest of the way.
Act as if everything is already okay.

SELF-LOVE PRINCIPLE #12

When a guy expresses doubt or hesitation
about being in an exclusive relationship with you,
this is not the time to step up and fill in the blanks for him.
You are responsible for writing your own life story—
not someone else's.

SELF-LOVE PRINCIPLE #13

Never chase after a man who says he doesn't know
what he wants. Real men go after what they want.

SELF-LOVE PRINCIPLE #14

Letting someone go is an act of love for yourself
and for the other person.

SELF-LOVE PRINCIPLE #15

Sexiness is not a title bestowed upon you from others.
It's an attitude and lifestyle you claim for yourself.

SELF-LOVE PRINCIPLE #16

Don't wait for a man to come and give you something
that you can give yourself.

SELF-LOVE PRINCIPLE #17

Focus your energy on vividly feeling how you would feel
when you have what you want most and you'll get it.

SELF-LOVE PRINCIPLE #18

**Honor your wants as much as your needs.
Ignoring the desires that make you unique
is self-sabotaging and serves no one.**

SELF-LOVE PRINCIPLE #19

**Neediness comes from a belief that the
answers to your problems lie within other people.
You have the answers to all your problems within you.**

SELF-LOVE PRINCIPLE #20

**Once you start treating yourself really well,
you won't accept anything less from others.**

SELF-LOVE PRINCIPLE #21

**Give yourself one experiential orgasm
and one physical orgasm a day.
Yes, every single day.**

SELF-LOVE PRINCIPLE #22

Don't dwell in a temporary funk. Give yourself
an instant dose of happy and go on about your day.
A happy woman is a sexy woman.

SELF-LOVE PRINCIPLE #23

Give yourself the gift of exploring your body
and learning what gives you pleasure
with and without a partner.

SELF-LOVE PRINCIPLE #24

Figure out what fun means to you and
make sure to have lots of it by yourself and
with people whose company you enjoy.

SELF-LOVE PRINCIPLE #25

A woman should always know how to protect,
take care of, and stand up for herself.

SELF-LOVE PRINCIPLE #26

**Protecting your physical and sexual health
is a powerful and necessary act of self-love.**

SELF-LOVE PRINCIPLE #27

**Get clear on what matters most to you
in a romantic relationship. Then make sure
you are living in that experience by yourself
before expecting that experience with a partner.**

SELF-LOVE PRINCIPLE #28

**Discovering and developing your passions
is a necessary act of self-love.**

SELF-LOVE PRINCIPLE #29

**A routine is not the same as an identity.
Break out of your routine to uncover your true identity.**

SELF-LOVE PRINCIPLE #30

The first step to knowing what you want
is knowing who you are.
Dedicate time to get to know yourself
and get clear on what you want.

SELF-LOVE PRINCIPLE #31

A lot of things are going to happen in your life.
There will be plenty of drama and unexpected challenges
to deal with. Don't look for or create drama
where drama isn't necessary.

SELF-LOVE PRINCIPLE #32

If you want different results in your love life,
you have to change the story that you are currently telling
to yourself and to other people.

SELF-LOVE PRINCIPLE #33

Focus on what you want rather than what you do not want.
Envision getting what you want as vividly as you can.

SELF-LOVE PRINCIPLE #34

Success is mastering something that matters to you.

SELF-LOVE PRINCIPLE #35

All people have a God-given gift that, if nurtured, would blossom tremendously and change lives. Invest in nurturing and expressing your gift.

SELF-LOVE PRINCIPLE #36

When you learn of someone else's success, don't hate—celebrate! There's enough success to go around!

SELF-LOVE PRINCIPLE #37

Pursue your career goals with persistence regardless of what other people say, think, or do.

SELF-LOVE PRINCIPLE #38

By always doing your best, you can focus on the journey rather than worry about the outcome of your efforts.

SELF-LOVE PRINCIPLE #39

The willingness to identify what needs to be done, create a plan, and then execute that plan —even when it's not fun—will drive you to success.

SELF-LOVE PRINCIPLE #40

You are the person, the permission, the right time, and the sign you have been waiting for.

What Does the Phrase "Be Your Own Boyfriend" Mean to You?

No one is going to treat you better than you treat yourself.

— 34 years old, Austin, TX, single

It's better to be alone than to settle for crap.

— 29 years old, Atlanta, GA, married

Take yourself out to the movies, treat yourself out to dinner, treat yourself to shopping sprees, and basically just be nice to yourself.

— 28 years old, Austin, TX, in a relationship

The first thing I think of is something dirty.

— 28 years old, Los Angeles, CA, dating

Be happy with who you are. Make sure that you are complete so that when that right person does come around, you're ready and you're not looking to find Mr. Make Me Happy; you're looking to find someone who complements you and who will appreciate you for who you are."

— 29 years old, Atlanta, GA, married

Don't stress about being in a relationship, but be open to one.

— 30 years old, Dallas, TX, single

I think about dancing to music in my house by myself while my dog watches confused.

— 34 years old, Austin, TX, single

Be comfortable in your own life, in your own skin, and comfortable with your decisions.

— 28 years old, Charlotte, NC, engaged

You have your own internal sense of self-worth and support. You don't demand it from a man.

— 28 years old, Chapel Hill, NC , engaged

Love who you are and love unconditionally. Obviously, we can have goals to be better and improve ourselves. But who we are is who we are. And we're given this mind, body, and soul for a reason. We each have our own gift and we have to love ourselves deeply, unconditionally no matter what. That is so important, and it's a lot easier said than done sometimes.

— Eric Handler, cofounder of PositivelyPositive.com

You are responsible for filling yourself up with love. If you don't have unconditional love for yourself, you actually can't give it to somebody else.

— Christine Arylo, "Queen of Self-Love," inspirational catalyst, author of *Choosing ME before WE* and *Madly in Love with ME*

You've heard people talk about how they can't wait to get married so they can travel and do this and do that. And you want to tell them you shouldn't wait to be in a relationship to do that stuff. So I think being your own boyfriend is being comfortable in your own skin and not needing another person to validate you.

— Damon Young, coauthor of *Your Degrees Won't Keep You Warm at Night*, cofounder of VerySmartBrothas.com

BYOB Experts

Arielle Loren
Sexuality writer, documentary filmmaker, founder of *CORSET* magazine
corsetmagazine.com

Christine Arylo
"Queen of Self-Love," inspirational catalyst, author of *Choosing ME before WE* and *Madly in Love with ME*
christinearylo.com

Christine Hassler
Inspirational speaker, life coach, author of *20-Something, 20-Everything: A Quarter-Life Woman's Guide to Balance and Direction* and *20 Something Manifesto: Quarter-Lifers Speak Out About Who They are, What They Want, and How to Get It*
christinehassler.com

Debra Grayson
Founder of decor and event services company Bedazzled by Debra
(and she's my mother!)

Denise Antoon
President and founder of PR and social media firm Antoon Group
antoongroup.com

Recommended Reading and Viewing

Codependent No More: How to Stop Controlling Others and Start Caring for Yourself
Melody Beattie

Crazy Sexy Diet: Eat Your Veggies, Ignite Your Spark, and Live Like You Mean It!
Kris Carr

The Dip: A Little Book That Teaches You When to Quit (and When to Stick)
Seth Godin

Fat, Sick & Nearly Dead, a Joe Cross film

The Four Agreements: A Practical Guide to Personal Freedom
Don Miguel Ruiz

Men Are from Mars, Women Are from Venus: The Classic Guide to Understanding the Opposite Sex
John Gray

Money, and the Law of Attraction: Learning to Attract Wealth, Health, and Happiness
Esther and Jeremy Hicks

Think and Grow Rich: Your Key to Financial Wealth and Power
Napoleon Hill

The War of Art: Break Through the Blocks and Win Your Inner Creative Battles
Steven Pressfield

Why Men Love Bitches: From Doormat to Dreamgirl—A Woman's Guide to Holding Her Own in a Relationship
Sherry Argov

Special Thanks to Our Kickstarter Backers

Between December 3, 2012 and January 4, 2013, my team and I ran an all-or-nothing fundraising campaign through the crowdfunding platform Kickstarter. Our goal was to raise $10,000 to help pay for editing, layout, graphic design, marketing, and trademark expenses and to be able to send free copies of *Be Your Own Boyfriend* to 100 women's and multicultural student centers at colleges around the United States. Two hundred thirty people around the world—from Kerala, India to Brisbane, Australia; Kingston, Jamaica to Austin, Texas—gave a total of $11,771. I am immensely grateful to each and every person who pledged their hard-earned money to help make my dream come true. Below is a list of the people who helped make this book possible through their generous pledges of $100 or more, some of whom I've never met in person. Thank you for believing in me and the message of BYOB!

The *Be Your Own Boyfriend* $100+ Backers Club:

Akilah Rogers	Greg Wiles	Opiyo Okeyo
Anthony Viola	Jacqueline DuBose	Patricia A. McQuater
Ben Adams	Janice Brown	Selena Soo
Ben Rapalee	Kofi Domfeh	Shadiah Sigala
Catherine Shen	LaRuan A. Cole	Siti Syahwali
Dana Christiansen	Leah Walter	Stan Veuger
Debra Grayson	Lori K. Lopez	Stephanie Pow
Denise Antoon	M. Ricardo Townes	Verick Cornett
Dwayne A. Brown	Millie Lapidario	